ABC OF CHURCH MUSIC

ABC
OF CHURCH MUSIC

by
STEPHEN RHYS, 1926-
and 11
KING PALMER

CRESCENDO PUBLISHING COMPANY
Boston

Standard Book Number 87597-025-7
Library of Congress Card Number 73-83175
Printed in the United States of America

FOREWORD

It might seem that the whole pattern of Church music is changing drastically in our country; and with the difficulty of retaining boy choristers, of securing the services of qualified organists and choir-masters, and persuading tenors and basses to sing in church choirs, the changes that are now noticeable will certainly be accelerated. Those who are in touch with country parishes and small towns are aware that music in churches is often in a poor way, and less vigorous than it was a generation ago. In fact some churches seem to be existing still, in their music, on efforts that were made in previous generations.

Yet despite these appearances there remains a foundation of durable skill and devotion, of belief in the future and respect for the good traditions of the past. What a triumph it is to build and equip in this very Spring a new choir school for St. Paul's Cathedral! Somebody has had faith. And wherever such achievements are found they seem to spring from the enthusiasm of one individual or of a small group of people who have been inspired by such a person.

> One man with a dream, at pleasure,
>   Shall go forth and conquer a crown;
> And three with a new song's measure
>   Can trample a kingdom down.

Often enough, in Church music, these creative people are non-professional musicians: what they teach they have learnt by experience, and employ with a contagious enthusiasm that springs from faith and hope: and in dealing with their choristers and their clergy they often need charity as well.

The present book, written by two musicians of skill and varied experience, is an attempt to help all those who are interested in Church music, by supplying basic information, and directing attention to sources from which further guidance can be sought. The book is short, and does not pretend to be complete, but is surprisingly far-reaching in its scope. I don't agree with everything it says; yet I think the book will help, and I hope so, for the splendour

5

of our English heritage in Church music is great, and much wider than is generally realised. Among the anthems by Byrd and Gibbons and others there are masterpieces which seem nowadays to be more fully understood and valued outside the area of liturgical performance than they sometimes are within it; and there are in addition many other fine compositions belonging to more recent periods. Some of these works, moreover, are not too difficult for a small choir of unpretentious singers, provided that these singers are willing to work hard, are modest, and are intelligently guided. Even among the hymn tunes of *Hymns Ancient and Modern*, so often ignorantly ridiculed, one can find short compositions that any musician might be proud to have written — small masterpieces that are capable of exercising great influence, for perfection is perfection, whether it be in a great cathedral or in the tiny barn of a Cotswold farm. Gibbons' Song 34, for example, contains in its few bars a perfection that is unmistakable; the Wesley poem to which it is set is also fine; and a service in which this short hymn was well sung would be, for this one thing, a distinguished occasion.

I hope, therefore, that this book will fulfil the hopes of its authors, and guide people towards the choice of suitable music for their particular circumstances, while giving a sense of direction to the efforts of those who will prepare and perform this music, not only "in quires and places where they sing" but also in the increasing number of churches where the music is the privilege and responsibility of the whole congregation.

SIR THOMAS ARMSTRONG
31st January, 1967

CONTENTS

LIST OF ABBREVIATIONS

PUBLISHERS

Throughout this book, abbreviations are used for names of publishers, as shown below.

A.H. & C. = Ascherberg, Hopwood & Crew
Bay. & Fer. = Bayley & Ferguson
B. & H. = Boosey & Hawkes
Bos. = Bosworth
Breit. = Breitkopf & Härtel
Chap. = Chappell
Ches. = Chester
Cur. = Curwen
Hin. = Hinrichsen
Leng. = Lengnick
Nov. = Novello
O.U.P. = Oxford University Press
Pat. = Paterson's
Ric. = Ricordi
S. & B. = Stainer & Bell
Sch. = Schott
S.P.C.K. = Society for the Promotion of Christian Knowledge
U.M.P. = United Music Publishers
Univ. = Universal Edition

HYMN BOOKS

The following abbreviations are used:

A.H.B. = *Anglican Hymn Book* (1965)
A. & M. = *Hymns Ancient and Modern* (Standard edition, 1861)
A. & M. (*Rev.*) = *Hymns Ancient and Modern* (Revised edition, 1950)
B.H. = *The Baptist Hymn Book* (1962)
Ch. H. = *The Church Hymnary* (1927)

9

Cong. P. = *Congregational Praise* (1951)
E.H. = *The English Hymnal* (Revised edition, 1933)
M.H. = *The Methodist Hymn Book* (1933)
S. of P. = *Songs of Praise* (Revised edition, 1932)

INTRODUCTION AND ACKNOWLEDGEMENTS

It is the authors' hope that this book may be useful to organists, choirmasters, and Church musicians in general; also to many others who, in one way or another, are interested in the music of the Church.

An attempt has been made to treat the subject on an ecumenical basis, by comparing and discussing the musical ritual of most of the Protestant Churches of Britain, as well as that of the Roman Catholic Church. Whenever a statement may be applicable to Churches of more than one denomination, the authors have (they hope without giving offence) used the word "minister" to denote priest, vicar, Free Church minister, pastor, etc.

The authors offer their grateful thanks to Sir Thomas Armstrong, M.A., D.Mus.(Oxon.), F.R.C.M., Hon.F.R.C.O., Hon.F.T.C.L., for generously agreeing to write the Foreword to this book. There can be few who are better qualified to do so. Before becoming Principal of the Royal Academy of Music, Sir Thomas was organist of Exeter Cathedral, of Christ Church Cathedral, Oxford, and Choragus of Oxford University. He has also contributed some distinguished Church music.

Of the many others who have generously given help, advice and information, the authors' thanks are especially due to the Revd. C. E. Pocknee, A.K.C., D.Th., F.S.A., who has patiently read the entire manuscript and offered many valuable suggestions; the Revd. D. Rochford, of St. George's Cathedral, London, S.E.1, who has given much detailed help and advice on the Roman Catholic liturgy; and to Lieutenant-Colonel Skinner and Major Ray Steadman-Allen of the Salvation Army, who have provided friendly and useful assistance. Thanks are also due to Mr. A. N. Arnold, A.M.I.E.E., President of the Organ Club; Mr. Gerald L. Barnes, F.R.C.O., G.R.S.M., A.R.C.M., Chairman of the Baptist Music Society; Mr. D. J. Bathurst, organist of Twickenham Baptist Church; Mr. Douglas Coates, General Secretary, Incorporated Guild of Church Musicians; Mr. W. M. Coulthard, F.R.C.O., A.R.C.M., L.R.A.M., Honorary Secretary, Scottish Societies of Organists; Mr. R. J. Dabner, Honorary General

Secretary, The Gregorian Association; Mr. F. N. Davidson Kelly, Ll.B., S.S.C., Honorary Secretary, Church of Scotland Committee on Public Worship and Aids to Devotion; Mr. Peter Lea-Cox; the Revd. Wilfred J. Little, Secretary, The Hymn Society of Great Britain and Ireland; Mr. Hugh Marchant, Professor at the Royal Academy of Music; Mr. A. H. Morriss, Honorary Treasurer, London Association of Organists; the Revd. Desmond Morse-Boycott, St. Mary-of-the-Angels Song School Trust; Mr. Alan A. Neubert, Honorary General Secretary, Free Church Choir Union; the Provost of St. Andrew's Cathedral, Aberdeen (the Very Revd. A. E. Hodgkinson); Dr. Erik Routley, D.Phil., F.R.S.C.M.; Mr. Roderick Spencer, organist of St. John's Church, Putney; Mrs. Wilhelmina Stephens, for advice on Dutch Roman Catholic music; the Revd. D. W. A. Stride, M.A., Warden and Headmaster, St. Michael's College, Tenbury; Mr. J. Lyddon Thomas, organist of Thames Ditton Congregational Church; Mr. A. Ivan Thompson, Musical Director, The Guild of St. Gregory; Mother Wilson, Headmistress, Convent of the Sacred Heart, Tunbridge Wells, also the Incorporated Society of Organ Builders, for much valuable advice about the organ.

Finally, grateful thanks must go to Mr. Leonard Cutts and his staff at Messrs. Hodder and Stoughton Limited, for encouragement and help which have made the writing of this book a pleasant task.

CHAPTER ONE

THE PLACE OF MUSIC IN WORSHIP

From time immemorial, voices and instruments have been associated with dancing, ritual and worship. As early as 4000 B.C., in the temples of the Mesopotamian cities, music was provided by the temple musicians who, as well as singing, probably played upon instruments; they were directed by the precentor, whose duty it was to intone the liturgic songs and psalms.

We shall make no attempt to give a history of early Christian music; the blending of the Hebrew, Greek and Latin elements is fully considered in the first two volumes of *The New Oxford History of Music* (O.U.P.).*

PLAINSONG

In this country, music began to take shape as an art towards the end of the sixth century, when it found its way into the services of the Christian Church. It was then that Church music, as we know it, was brought to England by St. Augustine who, with forty monks, was sent there by Pope Gregory as a missionary. St. Augustine founded the first song-school in Thanet in 597, and became the first of the many Benedictine Archbishops of Canterbury. St. Augustine and his monks brought with them (on their lips) the Gregorian music which could not at that time be written down, because no satisfactory method of notation existed. Gregorian chant has come to be known as plainsong, though there are other forms of plainsong which are very much older, some of them probably pre-Christian. For three centuries (sixteenth to eighteenth) plainsong was debased and misunderstood; then, as a result of years of research by the monks of Solesmes (working for the Roman Church), the Plainsong and Mediaeval Society and others, the authentic style was "rediscovered", and

* Winfred Douglas's *Church Music in History and Practice* (Faber & Faber) gives an excellent overall picture of the development of Church music from earliest to modern times.

13

great efforts are being made today to improve the performance of plainsong.

Drama and music occupied an important place in the early Church (tenth to fourteenth centuries). To "instruct the people" many plays were performed in the church. Sometimes these plays were sung, chiefly in plainsong—with some instruments. Some of these plays (e.g. *The Play of Daniel* and *Herod*) are being unearthed today, and given performances in churches.

EARLY HARMONY

The earliest idea of harmony seems to have grown from the practice of singing the traditional plainsong in octaves instead of in unison, thus enabling boys and women to sing with men. Later, perhaps in the ninth or tenth centuries, it became common to sing a melody in two parallel parts, one of which was a perfect fifth or a perfect fourth below the other. This practice, known as *organum*, very possibly developed because a tenor melody which was transposed a fourth or fifth lower was more comfortable for basses; if the tenor and bass parts were then transposed an octave higher, they would suit sopranos and altos.

From organum in parallel fourths, fifths and octaves, there was a gradual movement towards part-writing which did not always maintain the same parallel intervals, and towards the admission of imperfect intervals (thirds, sixths, etc.). One of the first treatises on the use of intervals was by Guido d'Arezzo (eleventh century).

EARLY POLYPHONY

The word polyphony has the same meaning as counterpoint, but here we use it simply in the sense of combining two or more melodies which, though moving independently, fit satisfactorily together. (Conversely, in homophony one voice has the melody, while the other voices take simple harmonic, or supporting parts.)

One step towards the establishment of polyphonic writing was the addition of a *descant* to a melody. Descant is a word with several meanings, according to the period to which it applies; it is used here to denote a counter-melody which, from about the twelfth century, was often improvised above a plainsong melody (this, the principal melody, then became known by the Italian name of *Canto Fermo*).

The step from a single-line-melody form of composition (whether simple, hymn-like, or very ornate—and these types were well-developed in this first melodic period) to the art of combining melodies, must have been historically as large (if not larger) than the steps we are taking today from tonality to atonality.

Naturally this took time. Experiments were made, satisfactory and unsatisfactory (as they are today). Theoreticians decreed that, while octaves, fifths and fourths were "perfect" intervals, thirds and sixths were "imperfect" intervals, to be used sparingly. If one examines the music of this period, one finds composers who were not only breaking these newly-formed rules, but were also using unprepared seconds and sevenths. Some composers used highly mathematical forms of composition (canons, hockets*); others were more expressive. This field of music is being explored more fully today, and is being found to contain much fresh sound and original construction. Nor is the music inexpressive. It is suggested that some medieval music should be on the shelves of the church library, and in the chapter on that subject we append lists of composers in England, France, Holland and Italy, with suggestions of publishers from whom these works are obtainable.

Church musicians who know little of this early period cannot do better than to listen to the records in the series *The History of Music in Sound* (General Editor: Gerald Abraham). The records are issued by E.M.I. Records Limited, and there are accompanying booklets for each period, in which musical examples are printed (O.U.P.).

LATER POLYPHONY

The full flowering of polyphonic music may be said to have been attained by those composers who, in the sixteenth and seventeenth centuries, when principles of musical notation, harmony and

---

* In a *canon*, a melody is first introduced alone, and is then repeated by another voice (or voices) during the course of the original statement of the melody. *Hocket* (similar to the word "hiccup") is a medieval name for a composition in which the phrases are broken or interrupted by rests.

counterpoint had been more fully established, left us what has become a golden heritage of Church music.

The tremendous output of first-class music (secular and sacred) in England at this time, often labelled "Tudor Music", should not allow us to forget that there was a similar outpouring of first-class music in France, Germany, Holland and Italy. Perhaps the four greatest names are Palestrina (1526–1594), Vittoria (c. 1548–1611), Orlando di Lasso (c. 1532–1594) and William Byrd (1543–1623). Other great composers abroad include the two Gabrielis, J. Handl, Hassler, Schütz, Vecchi, Monterverdi—it is difficult to know where to stop. In England, the richer period is the latter half of Elizabeth's reign—Byrd, Morley (c. 1557–1603), Tomkins (c. 1572–1656), Weelkes (c. 1575–1623), and Gibbons (1583-1625). Dowland, Bull and Wilbye wrote little Church music. One must include Taverner, Tallis, Tye, Whyte, Farrant,* and there are many others. Most of this music has Latin words and needs translation if it is to be sung in the vernacular. Publishers usually provide a translation.

Our recommendation here is that while English composers should be represented in English churches, it is the best music of all lands, within the capacity of the choir, which should be performed.

THE REFORMATION

By the time of the Reformation, Church music had advanced to a high degree of perfection. The suppression of the monasteries (1536–1539) was undoubtedly a severe setback for English Church music, for even though cathedral music remained relatively undisturbed, the song schools which trained boys for the monastic choirs were deprived of their office. On the other hand, the Act of Uniformity of 1549, which ordered "the Book of Common Prayer and no other" to be used, necessitated the substitution of English for Latin in the Church services. The task of providing music for use in the Anglican Church, in place of the traditional Latin masses and motets, helped to lay the foundations for a "national" school of English Church music.

In 1550, John Merbecke (died c. 1585), organist of St. George's

---

* This list of preference ("greater" and "also ran") is that suggested by E. H. Fellowes in his *English Cathedral Music* (Methuen).

Chapel, Windsor Castle, adapted the ancient plainsong to the prayer book of Edward VI, modifying the plainsong to suit the accentuation of the English language, and adding some original music in plainsong style. Although, two years later, the revision of the prayer book meant that Merbecke's music could no longer be used, it has come into its own, some three centuries later, partly through Stainer's edition of *The Cathedral Prayer Book*, and later through better editions – e.g. Wyatt and Shore (Nov.).

Despite the efforts of Protestant extremists to abolish all polyphonic Church music, the old style was not discarded, but was often treated with greater simplicity. E. H. Fellowes (*English Cathedral Music*) paints a vivid picture of the composer of this period. Having developed great skill in the polyphonic style, he was suddenly called upon to produce very simple "block harmony" (all four parts moving together for the most part) for the English rite, on the basic Puritan principle of "a note to a syllable". This is the origin of those extremely simple anthems by such composers as Tye and Hilton, which are so useful to elementary choirs today. They were the first anthems in the vernacular. The psalms and canticles began to be set to Anglican chant; this was a simplified form of Gregorian chant, in which the tunes were harmonised and measured, although the rhythm could be modified to fit verses which were longer or shorter. The Anglican chant did not, however, really come into fashion until the Restoration.

THE COMMONWEALTH AND RESTORATION

The Puritan leaders were lovers of secular music, and had no objection to organs as domestic instruments. Their opposition to elaborate Church music, however, led to the destruction of organs and music libraries in cathedrals and churches. After a break of eleven years (1649-1660), when the churches began the task of restoration, the cathedral choir schools were empty, and of the new choirmen at the Chapel Royal only five remembered the old traditions of singing the services. The choirboys at the Chapel Royal were put under the charge of Captain Henry Cooke. This Captain Cooke must have been one of the world's most successful choirmasters. Amongst his boys he had no less than five composers whose names are known to posterity: John Blow, Henry Purcell, Pelham Humphrey, Michael Wise and Thomas Tudway.

Pelham Humphrey (1647-1674) married Cooke's daughter, and upon Cooke's death succeeded him as Master of the Children of the Chapel Royal. At seventeen, Humphrey was sent abroad by Charles II to continue his studies: on his return he was put in charge of the band of twenty-four violins with which the King had provided himself; this band took part in anthem performances which had been secularised.

John Blow (?1648-1708) was appointed organist at Westminster Abbey at the age of nineteen, and on the death of Humphrey he succeeded him as Master of the Children. Blow who, so far as is known, was the earliest musician to receive the Lambeth degree of Doctor of Music, resigned his post at the Abbey in 1679, and was succeeded by his twenty-year-old pupil Henry Purcell. Blow wrote many anthems (some for special occasions) and other Church music, much of which shows considerable harmonic inventiveness.

Michael Wise (c. 1648-1687), who became organist and Master of the choristers at Salisbury, wrote several anthems and services.

Thomas Tudway (1650-1726) wrote anthems and a *Te Deum* for the consecration of Lord Oxford's private chapel at Wimpole.

Henry Purcell (c. 1658-1695) became keeper and tuner of the royal organs, virginals, recorders and other wind instruments, in addition to his position as organist at Westminster Abbey. He wrote a large amount of Church music, theatre music, royal odes and instrumental music. In the complete works of Purcell (Nov.) there are several volumes of anthems. Many of these take the form of Verse Anthems, of which the well-known "Bell Anthem" ("Rejoice in the Lord Alway") is a typical example. The anthem is cast in several sections; short instrumental *ritornelli* (interludes) alternate with vocal trios, solos, quartets and choruses. Purcell's anthems frequently end with an extensive *Alleluya*; some are rather long, but they should certainly be more used than they are today.

Abroad, the Danish organist and composer Buxtehude (1637-1707) —J. S. Bach walked two hundred miles to hear him play the organ—produced some fine Church cantatas and organ music. As he was organist of a sailor's church, the music was fresh and simple, often dance-like; a breath of fresh air after some heavy devotional music.

The best sacred music of the early part of the eighteenth century is by J. S. Bach and Handel (both born in 1685). The fact that Handel spent part of his life in England is often given as the reason for the great poverty of English music after the death of Purcell.

J. S. Bach's two hundred extant Church cantatas are being more widely used in our churches today; choruses, chorales, etc., can be extracted from these wonderful works *ad infinitum*. Some of the solos are perhaps a little too introspective for the average pragmatic Anglo-Saxon. The great Passions, the Mass in B Minor, etc., can be performed by combined choirs on Good Friday and other occasions. Many of our best hymn tunes are chorales arranged by J. S. Bach.

Handel's oratorios have been well used for some time, and are more familiar to the average Britisher. Nevertheless, the quality of the music has stood the test of time; the architecture, the sense of contrast, the beautiful melodies. *Messiah* is still performed at least a hundred times a year in Great Britain by amateur choral societies.

In the latter half of the eighteenth century, Haydn (1732–1809) began life as a choirboy. He wrote fourteen masses, some of which are very fine (e.g. the "Nelson" Mass). His oratorio *The Creation* is another work which is very well known to English audiences. Nor can we forget the *Austrian Hymn*, also used in his "Emperor" Quartet.

Mozart (1756–1791), amongst his enormous output wrote twelve masses, the motet* "Ave, verum corpus" and a Requiem, his last work, which he was unable to finish.

In England there is still a certain amount of prejudice against works such as the masses of Haydn and Mozart. Even the enlightened *Oxford Companion to Music* (Percy Scholes—O.U.P.) dismisses these works as lacking "the devotional quality of those of a century-and-a-half earlier". Be this as it may, there are many "devotional" works which the average churchgoer finds rather tedious; the masses of Mozart and Haydn have a freshness, a natural joy and sometimes a deep seriousness (cf. Mozart's

---

* The early motet was a sacred vocal composition in contrapuntal style, and usually unaccompanied; later it developed into a polyphonic work generally set to Latin words. In the Anglican Church its place was taken by the anthem.

Requiem, Haydn's "Nelson" Mass) which remind one of the wonderful saying of Christ: "Except ye become as little children . . ."

It is almost impossible now to list adequately the names of the great composers of Church music abroad, so with a passing and totally inadequate reference to Pergolesi (1710–1736), whose *Stabat Mater* for treble voices is a perennial delight, and to Vivaldi (1675–1741), we move to the Anglican Church composers.

William Croft (1678–1727) is chiefly known for his setting of the Burial Service, the opening sentences of which have remarkable beauty. Croft was also responsible for such vigorous hymn tunes as *St. Anne* and *Hanover* (*E.H.* Nos. 450 and 466).

John Weldon (1676–1736), who succeeded John Blow as organist of the Chapel Royal, is best known for his anthems "Hear my crying" and "In thee, O Lord, have I put my trust".

Maurice Greene (*c.* 1694–1755) was organist of St. Paul's Cathedral and the Chapel Royal, and Professor of Music at Cambridge University. The style of his music was to some extent influenced by that of his great friend Handel; of his many anthems some of the full ones, such as "Lord, let me know mine end" (which was sung at Nelson's funeral), are among the better works of the period.

William Boyce (1710–1779) became an articled pupil of Maurice Greene. He was appointed composer to the Chapel Royal, and conductor of the Three Choirs Festival (Gloucester, Worcester, Hereford). As well as his Church music, Boyce wrote a quantity of music for the theatre and pleasure gardens (of which the best known is probably his "Heart of Oak"). Some of his many anthems and services are still widely used—they include "The Lord is King", "Turn Thee unto me, O Lord", and "O where shall wisdom be found?" Boyce's greatest contribution to Church music is, however, the three volumes of *Cathedral Music*. This collection, which covers two centuries of Church music by English composers, was started by Maurice Greene from material supplied by John Alcock (1715–1806) the organist and composer; Boyce completed the collection which Greene had left unfinished at the date of his death.

Jonathan Battishill (1736–1801) is chiefly remembered for two short but expressive anthems "O Lord, look down from heaven" and "Call to remembrance".

The Book of Common Prayer of 1662 had left the Nonconformists in no doubt that they were to be excluded from the established Church. They therefore set to work to produce Church music of their own.

From the middle of the sixteenth century to the beginning of the eighteenth, many books of psalm words and psalm tunes were brought back from Geneva by divines who had fled there from England and Scotland to escape persecution. Calvinism, which flourished in Geneva, allowed congregational singing of metrical versions of the psalms, but not of "human hymns". Lutheranism, which on the Continent flourished side by side with Calvinism, did not gain a foothold in this country. Lutheran practice allowed the singing of hymns; Luther himself, like General Booth some three centuries later, appreciated the value of tunes with a popular appeal, and wondered why "the devil should have all the best tunes". But despite the flowering of English hymnody, the propriety of allowing hymn-singing was a matter of bitter controversy among the supporters of many denominations; Scottish churches, in particular, did not allow the singing of hymns until near the end of the nineteenth century.

The cradle of the modern hymn was Congregationalism; it was the Independents (later to be called Congregationalists) who, with the Methodists, took the forward path which led to the adoption of hymns as the musical framework of most Nonconformist services.

Three men who provided hymns in abundance were Isaac Watts, and Charles and John Wesley. Isaac Watts (1674–1748) was the son of a leading Dissenter who went to prison for his Nonconformity. Watts, who has been called the "father of English hymnody", published in 1707 *A Short Essay Toward the Improvement of Psalmody* in which he sets forth his principles for Congregational praise; these principles were embodied in his *Hymns and Spiritual Songs* (1707–1709). Watts was the author of hundreds of hymns; those which are sung today include "Our God, our help in ages past" (altered to "O God" by John Wesley).

Charles Wesley (1707–1788) became a college tutor at Christ Church, Oxford, where he founded a group of "Methodists". He was ordained, and proved himself an enthusiastic and effective evangelist. He was the author of more than six thousand hymns, most of which grew out of the Methodist revival; they include such favourites as "Hark, how all the welkin rings" (known more commonly today as "Hark! the herald angels sing"), "O for a thousand tongues to sing", and "Jesu, Lover of my soul".

John Wesley (1703–1791) took Holy Orders, and after acting for a short time as curate to his father, the Revd. Samuel Wesley, went with his brother Charles to Georgia, where he became resident minister for the Society for the Propagation of the Gospel. At this time he came into contact with a group of Moravian monks, under whose influence he took to vegetarianism and started to learn German. A few years later he experienced a "conversion", left the Moravians, and devoted himself to evangelism; during the course of his preaching he travelled more than two hundred thousand miles. In 1737 Wesley published, in Georgia, his *Psalms and Hymns* which, with its metrical psalms, translations from the German and Greek, and original hymns by the Wesley brothers, became the first of the modern-style hymn books.

THE EARLY NINETEENTH CENTURY

The history of Anglican Church music was at a very low ebb at the beginning of the nineteenth century. In many cathedrals the choirs were feeble and badly paid; some of the clergy, though receiving good stipends, did not always attend the services. In village churches, the singing was often led by a village orchestra from the west gallery—and while this activity must have been good for the musical life of the village, as an aid to devotion it may have been questionable. Scholes says: "In 1802 Bangor Cathedral possessed no choir, although the bishop's stipend was £6,000 p.a." (*The Oxford Companion to Music.*)

The singing of hymns was introduced at this time into the services of the Church of England, due to the efforts initially of Thomas Cotterill of Sheffield, and of James Montgomery.

Partly due to heroic work on the part of musicians such as S. S. Wesley (1810–1876) and Stainer (1840–1901), and partly due to the Oxford Movement, conditions began to improve. By 1870 church choirboys were receiving an adequate education, and the cathedrals were improving standards of repertoire and performance.

This low period in sacred music coincides with a huge outpouring of music outside the Church. The romantic period was beginning with a greater accentuation on feeling as opposed to form. Chopin and Schumann wrote almost no sacred music, but one of the finest masses of all time—Beethoven's *Missa Solemnis* (1818–1823)—was published. This music is not, however, intended for inclusion within a Church service: though there is no reason why it should not be performed in a church if resources are available. The practice of writing masses for concert performance was at last forbidden by Pope Pius X in 1903. Schubert, Cherubini, Weber, and others wrote many such masses.

Mendelssohn (1809–1847) wrote a considerable amount of sacred music. His music is sometimes considered sentimental or facile, but the pendulum of opinion is beginning to swing the other way—this is a very superficial account of a great composer. His *Elijah* (with *Messiah* and *The Creation*) is one of the three most performed serious sacred cantatas in this country. Mendelssohn wrote many other sacred oratorios (*St. Paul, Lobgesang*, etc.), and anthems. His style of composition was often copied by inferior composers with tawdry results; but this has happened at all periods to all composers. Mendelssohn was also largely responsible for "re-discovering" the music of J. S. Bach.

Gounod (1818–1893), the French composer, went to Rome to study older Church music, but produced a type of Church music nearer to opera; this, with the music of Spohr (1784–1859) encouraged many imitators, with unfortunate results.

The feebleness of English Church music composed at this time must be partly blamed on the would-be performers; i.e. the church choirs, as well as on the lack of native talent. Composers are, as a rule, largely inspired by performers, and the thought that an anthem would get a poor performance is not much inducement to writing one.

Samuel Wesley (1766–1837), the son of Charles Wesley, was a gifted composer, and was considered one of the finest organists of his day. As a young man he joined the Church of Rome for a time, and three years later he met with a street accident which left him subject to mental disturbance at intervals. His output of Church music is small but some of his anthems, such as "In exitu Israel" (for double chorus) show considerable originality. Wesley's son, Samuel Sebastian (1810–1876), who was also very distinguished as an organist, wrote a good deal of Church music of considerable quality. "Blessed be the God and Father", "Wash

23

me throughly", and "Lead me Lord" are among his most expressive anthems. His hymn tunes include the popular *Aurelia* (*E.H.* No. 489).

Thomas Attwood (1765-1838), after beginning his career as a chorister of the Chapel Royal, went to Vienna as a pupil of Mozart. Some of his smaller works are still sung; among them the anthems "Teach me, O Lord" and "Come, Holy Ghost".

William Crotch (1775-1847), the infant prodigy who at four years old was giving organ recitals in London, left some useful short anthems: e.g. "Lo, star-led chiefs" (for Epiphany-tide).

Thomas Attwood Walmisley (1814-1856) was an able organist and composer. His Evening Service in D Minor remains one of the better services in the English cathedral tradition.

Other lesser composers of the century include Henry Smart (1810-1879), who is chiefly remembered for his hymn tunes (e.g. *Heathlands* and *Regent Square*, *E.H.* Nos. 395 and 431); William Sterndale Bennett (1816-1875) who wrote a few anthems; and Frederick Gore Ouseley (1825-1889) who, before he was thirty, had begun to establish St. Michael's College, Tenbury (see page 169); of Ouseley's many services and anthems "How goodly are thy tents" is one of the best.

These and other early Victorian composers produced a considerable amount of Church music, and in this they were aided (1) by the cheap octavo editions produced by Novello and Company, the music publishers, and (2) by the activities of the Oxford Movement, dating from 1833, which led to the establishment of surpliced choirs in many churches, and to an increased demand for services and anthems.

In the mid-Victorian period, English composers such as Barnby, Stainer and Sullivan came under the foreign influence of Mendelssohn, Spohr and Gounod, whose Church music (especially that of Spohr and Gounod) was too often of inferior quality. John Stainer was certainly the most distinguished of the group. An outstanding organist and accompanist, he composed the large-scale choral work *The Crucifixion*, which has enjoyed great popularity. If his work is now a little dated, one must not forget his huge efforts in the Anglican Church at raising standards of repertory and performance.

Joseph Barnby (1838-1896) was a great choral conductor who succeeded Gounod as conductor of the Albert Hall Choral

Society. A few of his anthems, chants and hymns are still used today.

Arthur Seymour Sullivan (1842–1900) sang as a boy in the Chapel Royal choir. His greatest gifts were as a composer of light opera, but he also wrote much sacred music. His vigorous setting of "Onward, Christian soldiers" (*St. Gertrude*) is one of the more powerful Congregational hymns. (How many people have noticed the imitation of the melody in the tenor part?)

John Bacchus Dykes (1823–1876) is chiefly known as a writer of hymns which are to be found in profusion in nearly all hymn books. If the harmonies are Victorian, the melodies are sound, and the appeal of such tunes as *Nicaea, Hollingside* and *Horbury* (*E.H.* Nos. 162, 414 and 444) will probably continue for some time.

The year 1861 saw the publication of the first full music edition of *Hymns Ancient and Modern* with 273 hymns, to which 113 hymns were added in the edition of 1868; *Hymns Ancient and Modern* was accepted without question as the most important collection of hymns in the English language, until its position began to be challenged by *The English Hymnal,* published in 1906, which exerted its influence over the hymnody of all denominations.

THE NINETEENTH–TWENTIETH CENTURY RENAISSANCE

Except for the five years of Queen Mary's reign (1553–1558) the Roman Catholic Church in Britain was regarded as heretical from the time of the Reformation (1534), and was only able to function properly in the chapels belonging to the Foreign Embassies. After the Catholic Emancipation Bill of 1829, the Church gradually became more legalised, and the quality of the music improved under men such as Samuel Webbe (father and son) and Vincent Novello (also the music publisher). In 1901 the Roman Catholic Cathedral in Westminster was built, and Richard Runciman Terry (1865–1938) became its first organist. Terry revived much early music (Palestrina, etc.) as well as early English Church music, and composed masses, motets, and hymn tunes. He published two volumes of psalms — the tunes harmonised by himself — *Calvin's First Psalter* (1932) and the *Scottish Psalter of 1635* (1935). He also edited the music of *The Westminster Hymnal* (see page 54).

The latter part of the nineteenth century, and the first decade or two of the twentieth, witnessed a great revival of English Church music. The two composers who set this new creative force in motion were Hubert Parry (1848–1918) and Charles Villiers Stanford (1852–1924). Parry was essentially an English composer, and one of his finest works is his eight-part setting of Milton's poem "Blest pair of sirens". Parry's splendid anthem "I was glad when they said unto me" was composed for the coronation of Edward VII, and repeated at other coronations. Another fine anthem is "Hear my words, ye people" for soprano and bass soli and chorus. There are some services which are in occasional use, and several broad hymn tunes which are deservedly popular, such as *Laudate Dominum, Repton*, and *Jerusalem (A. & M. (Rev.)* Nos. 376, 184 and 578).

Stanford was born in Dublin, and became Professor of Music at Cambridge. His Service in B Flat, an early work, attracted great interest, especially as Stanford made use of "Gregorian Intonations" in some parts of the work, using them with skill and imagination. The Service in C Major (his last) is usually regarded as his best, but several of his other settings are still used. Nearly all of Stanford's anthems and motets show his skilful craftsmanship; but though his hymn tunes are always interesting, they lack the "congregational quality" which is to be found in Parry's hymn tunes.

During the last three decades of the nineteenth century, a collection of "gospel" or "mission" hymns was brought from the U.S.A. by the evangelistic singer Ira D. Sankey (1840–1908) who, with D. L. Moody, toured this country. A large collection of hymns, many with tunes by Sankey, were published under the title *Sacred Songs and Solos* (1874). The words of these hymns were set to "catchy" melodies, often of the verse/refrain type; the rhythm was ordinary and the harmony poverty-stricken. Nevertheless, these hymns found great popular appeal, and many hymns of this type were taken up by The Salvation Army (founded by William Booth in 1878). Some of Sankey's better tunes are still to be found in most hymn books (e.g. *The Ninety and Nine*, said to be the best tune Sankey ever wrote — *E.H.* No. 584, and *B.H.* No. 425). *B.H.* also contains *Shelter* (No. 566).

Following Parry and Stanford, we come to a considerable group of composers born between 1850 and 1900, about whose music we have space to include only the briefest comments.

26

Edward Elgar (1857–1934) wrote a few anthems, and also a few chants of quality; some movements from oratorios (*The Dream of Gerontius, The Kingdom,* etc.) have also been published.

Basil Harwood (1859–1949), organist and composer of anthems and larger works, displayed craftsmanship and an effective style.

Walter Galpin Alcock (1861–1947), organist and composer; his Church music includes an excellent Morning and Evening Service in B Flat, and several large anthems. He also wrote *The Organ* (Nov.), a very useful primer for beginning organists.

Alfred Hollins (1865–1942), blind organist and composer of several anthems, mostly for Harvest, Easter and Christmas.

Charles Wood (1866–1926) studied organ with Stanford, and succeeded him as Professor of Music at Cambridge. He wrote many notable services and anthems, also some fine hymns (e.g. *Rangoon* and *Cambridge, Cong. P.* Nos. 338 and 757). There is also an interesting Passion, based on plainsong.

Walford Davies (1869–1941) was organist of St. George's Chapel, Windsor Castle, conductor of the Bach Choir, Musical Director of the Royal Air Force (1914–1918), and Master of the King's Musick. He composed many Church services, anthems and hymns, most of which display his characteristic "rising sixth" and (in his hymns) the "filling out" of the final chords. His hymn "God be in my head" (*Cong. P.* No. 745) is a good illustration of the use of the rising sixth, which is also to be found in works such as *Solemn Melody* and the *R.A.F. March Past.* He was a man of great devotion.

Vaughan Williams (1872–1958) was a great English composer who made a considerable contribution to the revival of English hymnody by musically editing *The English Hymnal* (1906 and 1933), *Songs of Praise* (1926 and 1932), and *The Oxford Book of Carols* (1928). For the last two he was joint editor with Martin Shaw, and to all three books he made some notable contributions, including some splendid descants (e.g. *Down Ampney, E.H.* No. 152; *King's Weston, S. of P.* No. 392; *Wither's Rocking Hymn, The Oxford Book of Carols* No. 185). He also composed some large-scale choral works (e.g. Mass in G Minor; *Hodie*), and many services and anthems. His musical discoveries in the field of folk song and modes, etc., all became incorporated into his sacred music.

Gustav Holst (1874–1934), pupil of Stanford, trombonist,

director of music at St. Paul's Girl's School and at Morley College, contributed some notable hymns (e.g. *Cranham, E.H.* No. 25; *Hill Crest, S. of P.* No. 86; *Monk Street, S. of P.* No. 534; and *Thaxted, S. of P.* No. 319, which was borrowed for *The Planets* (*Jupiter*). His religious views, however, tended towards the East.

Sydney Nicholson (1875–1947), organist at Westminster Abbey, founder of The School of English Church Music (see page 159), and author of *Quires and Places Where They Sing* (S.P.C.K.), was editor of *The Parish Psalter* (see page 37) and "assessor" of *Hymns Ancient and Modern* (Rev. 1950), to which he contributed many hymns (e.g. *Aethelwold*, No. 143; *Bow Brickhill*, No. 215; *Feniton*, No. 392).

Geoffrey Shaw (1876–1958) was organist and composer of many Church services, anthems and hymns (e.g. *Paddocks, Praise, Water-End, Gillam — S. of P.* Nos. 402, 499, 624, 649).

Martin Shaw (1876–1958), organist and composer, and brother of the above, was joint editor (with Vaughan Williams) of *Songs of Praise* and *The Oxford Book of Carols*. His Church music includes *Folk Mass*, many services and anthems, and hymns such as *Oxenbridge, Bromley Common, Battle Song* and *Marching* (*S. of P.* Nos. 104, 187, 578, 678).

THE TWENTIETH CENTURY

An excellent survey of the Church music of this century will be found in Dr. Erik Routley's *Twentieth Century Church Music* (1964), the first of a series of "Studies in Church Music" to be published by Herbert Jenkins.

In the previous section we gave brief consideration to some composers of Church music who were born before the close of the last century. We shall make no attempt to discuss the music of composers who are still living, but shall be content to mention the names of a few of those who have made significant contributions to the literature of Church music.

Composers born between 1880 and 1900 include Sir Thomas Armstrong, Sir George Dyson, Sir William Harris, Herbert Howells, Gordon Jacob, Alec Rowley, W. K. Stanton, Heathcote Statham, Zoltan Kodály (Hungarian), Frank Martin (Swiss), Francis Poulenc (French), and Igor Stravinsky (Russian).

Composers born in 1900 or after include Lennox Berkeley,

Benjamin Britten, Donald Cashmore, Gordon Crosse, Peter Maxwell Davies, Gerald Finzi, Allan Hoddinott, John Joubert, Anthony Milner, Edmund Rubbra, Eric Thiman, Michael Tippett, William Walton, Lloyd Webber, Aaron Copland (U.S.A.), Jean Langlais, Olivier Messiaen (French), Flor Peeters (Belgian organist and composer), Ernest Pepping, H. W. Zimmermann (German), and Mátyás Seiber (Hungarian).

The twentieth century has seen the development of a new style of psalmody—midway between plainsong and Anglican chant—by the French Jesuit priest, Père Joseph Gélineau. It has also seen the introduction of the electronic organ into Church music, and some experimentation with "pop" and "light" music idioms, as well as serial and *avante-garde* styles.

Most hymn books have undergone a revision, and the various denominations have borrowed from each other, so that the books are becoming more similar. New chant books, new psalm books with new methods of pointing have appeared. But, above all, there has been a steady gradual improvement in the quality of the music in the ordinary parish and village church. Although many churches still have male-only choirs, others have now grown used to mixed choirs. The improvement is partly due to the work of The Royal School of Church Music, partly to radio and television, and partly to the individual organists and choirmasters who are taking their work more as a vocation than a hobby.

THE PLACE OF MUSIC IN WORSHIP

Church music, unlike secular concert music, is not an end in itself; it is only one of the external accessories—the psychological aids—to worship, and it must take its proper place in the general scheme. But though Church music may be cast in a supporting role, it must play its full part in helping the spiritual development of the worshipper.

"Is Jazz Music Christian?" asks Dr. Erik Routley,* and answers "No, it is not Christian, nor is any other kind of music." Music is only Christian music, or Church music, in so far as it enables Christians to enter more fully into the worship of God. The test of Church music, therefore, must be not only whether,

* *Is Jazz Music Christian?* Pamphlet by Erik Routley (Epworth Press, 1964).

as music, it is good or bad, but also whether, as music, it is appropriate in character to the spirit of the service for which it is intended (whether this be Roman Mass, Anglican Evensong, or Salvation Army "Holiness" meeting); and whether, as music, it helps us to lift up our hearts, and brings us a little nearer to the glory of God. Many who have attended Quaker Meetings will have experienced the spiritual character of the silent worship which needs no music; they may also have experienced the unspiritual character of some other services, where the psalms and responses have been sung mechanically, and hymns with inappropriate words mouthed by an apathetic choir and congregation.

Music in church, as opposed to Church music, may be justified on wider grounds. For instance, a Bach fugue may give much pleasure to a congregation, and so great a work of art may leave many with hearts uplifted. It is when we come to the question of "good" music that we face the real problem. Of the greatness of some music there is little doubt, and of the badness of other music there may be even less doubt. But between the two there is a large tract of debatable land; and who shall say which of the seed has fallen on good ground, and which on stony?

Those who have the gifts of musical talent and appreciation may indeed rejoice at the glories they have inherited—the wealth of plainsong, polyphony and hymns which has been handed down to us, and the fine Church music of recent times. Other music they may regard as so impoverished that it will never lead towards spiritual health. Yet before we condemn as "unspeakably vulgar" certain Victorian and Nonconformist music, or as "tawdry" many of the hymns in the Sankey–Moody idiom, or even as "blatantly commercial" the use of "pop" or "jazz" idioms in liturgical music, perhaps we should reflect that we, the children of God, are "all sorts and conditions of men"; and that, for all we know, the music which is so easy to despise may sometimes lead a doubting Thomas to the feet of the Master.

CHAPTER TWO

PROSE SET TO MUSIC

Why set prose to music? Some less musical worshippers may feel that the spoken word is more effective without the support of music. A composer, however, having been inspired by words for which he has respect or affection, feels that he understands their emotional or dramatic force, and wishes to emphasise this in music, so that others are made more aware of this deeper significance. Good music has an enriching, even a mystical, effect on words. In time, the composer's insight percolates through to the worshipper, as the music becomes familiar, so that the passage becomes "flatter, duller" without the music.

As prose has irregular stress and irregular phrase-lengths, the music must either be irregular and fit the words exactly or it needs to have a very elastic form, capable of contraction and expansion. Plainsong is typical of the first method; the "Anglican chant" is a successful form for the second.

Plainsong is an enormous subject; for some people a life-study. It was formerly the exclusive province of the Roman Catholic Church, but today Anglican and Free Churches have begun to make use of the repertoire. Plainsong melodies themselves are of many kinds—from very simple to very ornate—from melodies with one note to one syllable to melodies with a great many notes to one syllable (*neumes* or *melismatas**). It is some of the simpler ones which have become familiar to non-Catholics. The more complicated ones are very beautiful, but possibly too difficult for congregational-type worship. The beauty lies in the melodic shape—the "up-and-downness of the notes"—like the contours of a range of mountains seen on the horizon. All good melodies have to some extent good "contours"; some have more subtle variation, some less. The best plainsong is often subtle (this may help to explain why some people get so excited about it).

Plainsong has very little "rhythm", and no regularly recurring

---

* *Neumes*, when combined in groups of two or more, were called *melismatas*.

beat. Some notes are twice as long, some three times, some are stressed and prolonged slightly; but basically all notes are equal in length. Plainsong has, however, a strong sense of "pulse"—it must not drag or rush, and it also has points of "impulse", from which the rhythm moves forward—less pronounced than a bar-line. The lack of rhythm (dotted rhythms, for example, are foreign to the art of plainsong) may make the subject seem a little too refined and remote from the ordinary man with his more primitive sense of rhythm (this may help to explain why some people have little or no interest in plainsong).

NOTATION OF PLAINSONG

The period from A.D. 800 to 1100 has been called "the golden years of plainsong". Much, or all, of this music which is known to us today might have been lost but for the timely intervention of a rational system of musical notation.

Our modern system of staff notation derives partly from alphabetic notation (which dates back to the early Greeks and Romans), and partly from neumatic notation. In the latter system, which was in use when Gregorian chant was first written down, the neumes (a series of dots, dashes and curves) were used not to indicate pitch or duration of sound, but to give a general idea of the rhythm, phrasing, and sometimes expression of melodies which had already been learnt by heart. Up to about the tenth century, alphabetic and neumatic notations were often combined. During the ninth and tenth centuries the idea was evolved of a notation in which the neumes were placed on a stave of two or more lines, each of which represented a different note. Later the neumatic signs were replaced by the square and other notes which have become familiar in the plainsong which is printed today. It is not certain whether these notes had rhythmic values; a considerable amount of discussion is being carried on today on this subject.* The normal practice today is to treat squares, diamonds, etc., as all of the same rhythmic value. Plainsong may therefore be looked upon as "prose music".

Plainsong uses a four-line stave, with a movable clef. The note

* J. W. A. Vollaerts, in his *Rhythmic Proportions in Early Medieval Chant* (Leiden, 1958), deals with the theory that plainsong notes had different values. Vollaerts's theory has not, however, been generally accepted.

between the arms of the clef may be considered as C. If, however, the pitch of the music lies too high or too low, the music may be transposed into any suitable key. The basic notes are all equal in length (see (a) below).* If two (or more) notes are written on top of each other, one reads from bottom to top, as indicated by the arrow in (b); otherwise one reads from top to bottom, as in (c). The little mark under some notes (d) is known as an "ictus"; it is the point from which the rhythm receives a forward impulse.

(a) ■ ▮ ♦   (c) ⟍ Read

(b) ⬛ ↑ Read   (d) ─▪─

This point may often occur on a weak syllable, and tends to smooth out the flow of words and music, as shown below.

Di-es Ir-ae, Di-es Il-la

Verbal stresses: <u>Di</u>,   <u>Ir</u> , <u>Di</u> <u>Il</u>
Musical stresses: <u>es</u> <u>ae</u>,   <u>es</u> . <u>la</u>

Net result: all syllables equal.

In order to keep the onward flow as smooth as possible, breaths are taken quickly; the first sign in the example below means a slight breath without a break (if possible); the second means a pause for a breath (of about one beat).

The accompaniment of plainsong is dealt with in Chapter Three. Although the accompaniment should be light, one must remember that what is "correct" may not be "effective"; and that the accompaniment will also depend on the quality of the choir, and the singing of the congregation. Plainsong may, of course, be unaccompanied.

An Anglican or Free Church organist might occasionally be called upon to play for a Roman Catholic service with plainsong. The following points might then be found useful: (1) If possible, ask to see everything in advance. (2) Sing through the melodies at home (remembering that the note between the arms of the clef

---

* Some historians are, however, beginning to question this.

can be considered as C). Decide if they lie too high or too low. This may depend on whether the particular section is to be sung by a minister with a tenor, baritone or bass voice; or by the choir (which may or may not have men's voices); or by everybody together. If a melody lies too high or too low, it should be transposed to another key. If you are bad at transposing, write it out— it will not take too long, and the act of writing it out will also fix it a little better in the memory. (3) Decide what chords to use and when to change them; practice playing and singing as you play. If necessary, write it all out. This will take time, but no one could pretend that it is easy to play for this music when the melodies are unfamiliar. (4) Look out for various signs which mean "priest only", "repeat this section"—the actual signs used vary slightly from book to book. Generally, V = minister, R = congregation (or choir). (5) Insist that someone sits beside you, armed with all the necessary books, and tells you exactly what to do, and always, if in doubt, do *not* play. A little gap is better than a *ff* chord in the middle of a prayer.

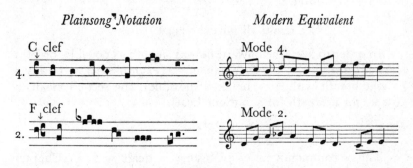

Plainsong Notation   *Modern Equivalent*

MODES

All medieval Church music is based upon a system of eight scales which are known as *Modes* (sometimes called Church modes, Ecclesiastical modes, or Gregorian tones). These modes, each of which has its individual character which is reflected in the mood of the chant to which it is applied, are possibly derived from Greek scales. They may be heard by playing on the piano or organ eight consecutive white keys; first D to D, then E to E, and so on as far as the next D to D; the notes of the eighth mode are the same as those of the first, though this is the only similarity between the two modes. Although seven of the modes begin on

34

different notes, there are normally only four "finals" (or, as we might say, tonics or key-notes) on which the chant ends. So we have four pairs of modes, with each of a pair *ending* on the same note but having different characteristics. As well as a final, each mode has a dominant (not always the fifth of the scale as in modern music), which becomes (1) a pivot around which the melody moves, and (2) a reciting note on which the greater part of each verse of the chant is recited.

In the early Church, considerable confusion arose as each individual church had its own musical ritual. St. Ambrose, Bishop of Milan (fourth century), and later Pope Gregory (sixth century) attempted to organise and classify the modes then in existence; hence the phrases "Ambrosian chant" and "Gregorian chant". Each mode, as well as having a final and a dominant, had a basic range of an octave. If this range reached from final to final, the mode was called Authentic; if from fifth to fifth, the mode was Plagal.

Modes are not exclusive to Church music. Outside the Church, the minstrels, troubadours, etc., were composing and performing music in the same systems. The recent explorations of composers such as Vaughan Williams, Bartok, etc., have unearthed much "folk music" which was written in modal scales.

Authentic modes (Range: Final–Final)

No.	Name	Authentic scale	Final	Dominant
1	Dorian	D–D	D	A
3	Phrygian	E–E	E	C
5	Lydian	F–F	F	C
7	Mixo-Lydian	G–G	G	D

Plagal modes (Range: Fifth–Fifth)

No.	Name	Plagal scale	Final	Dominant
2	Hypodorian	A–A	D	F
4	Hypophrygian	B–B	E	A
6	Hypolydian	C–C	F	A
8	Hypomixo-Lydian	D–D	G	C

If these scales are played on the piano or organ, it will be apparent that the difference between one mode and another lies in the arrangement of the order of tones and semitones; since any of the scales may be transposed, the difference is not that of pitch but of "flavour".

35

If it is desired to add a modal accompaniment to a plainsong melody, only the notes of the particular mode should be used, with one exception; B flat may be substituted for B natural if desired.

TIME-SIGNATURES AND CLEFS

Time-signatures were adopted about the fourteenth century, and bar-lines gradually came into use during the next two centuries; proportional notes were also adopted which were not unlike those in use today. The number of the lines of the stave was eventually fixed at five, and clefs (which had at first appeared in the neume system) were used both in a fixed form (G or treble clef, and F or bass clef), and in a movable form (C clef, placed on the bottom line of the stave became the soprano clef; on the third line the alto clef; and on the fourth line the tenor clef).

ANGLICAN CHANT

Another method of setting prose to music is the elastic Anglican chant. The typical form is described in detail in Chapter Six. The single chant consists of R 2B E–R 4B E: where R = reciting note, B = notes between bar-lines (2B = two notes between bar-lines), E = ending note. The double chant repeats this pattern twice: the quadruple four times. Basically, Anglicans use single and double chants – short psalms can have single chants and longer psalms double chants; longer psalms may even change the chant at some suitable point where the mood or sense of the psalm changes. The canticle *Te Deum* has two very marked points where the sense changes, and is usually sung to three chants. There is a certain amount of liturgical discussion about where these points of change should be; the present arrangement seems to be a nineteenth-century mistake, and the sections should be 1–13: 14–21: and 22–end. When chants change there must be some key-relationship between the chants – and the choir must practice the point of change very thoroughly. If this is done inefficiently the congregation will groan inwardly. There is a very amusing caricature of bad psalm singing which lively curates produce at Christmas revues, and included in this is a delicious "wrench" when the chant changes ("just as the congregation has got used to the first tune").

There are many different chant books, including the three which go with *The New Cathedral Psalter* (Nov.); *The Anglican Chant Book* (Nov., 1955); *The Oxford Chant Books* Nos. 1 and 2, edited by Stanley Roper, Arthur Walker and Henry Ley (O.U.P.); and *The Oxford Chant Book for Three-Part Singing*, edited by Henry Coleman (O.U.P.); these last three books are specially suitable for school worship.

Some of the main psalters are:

The Cathedral Prayer Book, edited by Stainer (Nov. 1891).

The New Cathedral Psalter, edited by Cosmo Lang (Archbishop of York), Charles Lloyd (Precentor of Eton), H. S. Holland (Canon and Precentor, St. Paul's), and George C. Martin (Organist of St. Paul's) (Nov., N.D.).

The Psalter Newly Pointed (S.P.C.K., 1925).

The Scottish Psalter (O.U.P., 1929).

The Parish Psalter, edited by Sir Sydney Nicholson (Faith Press, 1928, with chants 1932).

The Oxford Psalter, edited by Henry G. Ley, E. Stanley Roper, and C. Hylton Stewart (O.U.P., 1929).

The Broadcast Psalter (S.P.C.K., 1949).

The Worcester Psalter, edited by Sir Ivor Atkins (A. & C. Black, 1948, new edn. 1963).

The Cathedral Prayer Book, followed by *The New Cathedral Psalter*, was one of the first "pointed" psalters, fitting the words of the psalms to the newly-developed Anglican chant. The words were split up into the "recitation" and the "portions between the bar-lines". A few dynamic markings appeared; e.g. *p*, *mf*, and *f*; but "the Editors did not advocate sudden or extreme dynamic changes in the interest of congregational singing". Commas were removed, and an asterisk (*) indicated that a fresh breath should be taken. If the psalm had an odd number of verses and a double chant was used, a note appeared in the margin—"use 2nd part" of the chant. The first important point was to have an agreed method by which one moved out of the recitation to the first note-change within the bar-lines. The method used was "gathering notes", when the congregation was "warned" that the first note-change was approaching. Three different printing methods were used to indicate this.

(1) They were organised into a single bar *a tempo* of a semibreve duration, this semibreve being split up in different ways according to the natural word-stresses, as shown in example (*a*) below.

(*a*) O Lo̊rd | save thy | people
        𝅗𝅥.   𝅘𝅥
       O Lord have | mercy. up- | on us
                ⌐—3—⌐
                𝅘𝅥 𝅘𝅥 𝅘𝅥
       He rode upon the cherubims | and did | fly

(2) They were marked with strong and weak stresses, as in prosody (see (*b*) below).

(*b*) O Lōrd | save thy̆ | people
       O Lōrd hă̆ve | mercy. up- | on us

(3) The last strong stress(es) before the bar-line were marked in heavy type, as in (*c*) below).

(*c*) O **Lord** | save thy | people
       O **Lord** have | mercy. up- | on us

As long as there were two syllables between each pair of barlines no special marks were needed, but when there were more than two syllables, the subdivision of the syllables was indicated by a dot or a hyphen: e.g. unto . the ("unto" sung to the first note, "the" to the second). A horizontal line (—) indicated that the preceding syllable was continued into the next bar:

        Go̊v |—ern | them

In the hands of a sensitive choirmaster and an intelligent choir good results could be produced by this method. But the method was open to abuse when used unintelligently. The editors of this psalter were well aware of the danger when they said: "Experienced choirmasters . . . do not require to be told that musical notes, in chanting, must be regarded as approximations, and are not intended to be sung with metronomic rigidity." Their aim

38

was that the "words may run smoothly and the sense be intelligible".

Owing to the unintelligent way in which the psalter was used, editors began to wonder if there were not better ways of pointing a psalter. The new cry was for "speech-rhythm", in which the words should flow along without unnatural interruptions. Various different psalters produced different methods, all with the same ideal in mind. This was to sing the psalm as it would be spoken by a professional reader. This involves using one's intelligence, ability to look ahead, feeling for the logic, drama, poetry, and above all for the natural rhythm of the words. All this—in addition to changing the note at the right time! Possibly with amateur choirs which can barely read music!

The editors of the speech-rhythm psalters therefore tried to discover some rules of good reading, which could be applied to the art of psalm singing, and tabulated as "methods".

"READ BEFORE YOU SING" (S.P.C.K. PSALTER)

The *S.P.C.K. Psalter Newly Pointed* was inspired by Robert Bridges —then Poet Laureate—and it has various suggestions for practising methods. Half the choir speaks the words deliberately; the other half sings, watching the lips of the first half. For the second verse the two halves change over. A second method is to read a verse, then repeat, singing to a monotone (or better to a four-part chord), and repeat a third time to a chant.

"A LINE TO A BREATH, AND NO HURRY" (S.P.C.K. PSALTER)
"UNHURRIED RECITATION AND CLEAR ARTICULATION" (WORCESTER PSALTER).

One needs to grasp the sense of a whole phrase or sentence, and sing this amount without a break—that is, without taking a breath. At the same time this must be clearly articulated without hurry; at first one must hold back the recitation and push on at the bar-lines until this becomes a natural process and the overall speed of words becomes even. The simplest way to indicate the quantity to be sung in one breath is to make one line of print equal to one breath, a method adopted by many psalters. Some psalters still prefer the asterisk.

A BAR-LINE (= CHANGE OF NOTE) TENDS TO GIVE THE FOLLOWING SYLLABLE A STRESS

This is perfectly natural, one's mind concentrating on the point of change, and one tends to stress the syllable. One of the aims of the editors of the speech-rhythm psalters was to alter the positions of the bar-lines so that the word-stress fell more naturally after the bar-line, as shown in example (*a*) given below.

(*a*)   *New Cathedral Psalter*   for vain | is the | help of | man

   cf. *Worcester Psalter*   for | vain. is the | help of | man

(Psalm 60:11)

However, it is sometimes very difficult to achieve this; it may involve putting a larger number of syllables between bar-lines, as in (*b*).

(*b*) *Oxford Psalter*   Through the tender | mercy of. our | God

(Benedictus)

The *S.P.C.K. Psalter* solves this problem by having two types of bar-line. The whole bar-line means that the following syllable *has* a stress: the half bar-line means that the note is changed as usual, but *without* stress, as shown in (*c*).

(*c*) *S.P.C.K. Psalter*   The Father ǀ ever | lasting

(Te Deum)

A GOOD READER WILL HURRY OVER SOME WORDS AND DWELL ON OTHERS

In fact, if words are spoken completely evenly, it is extremely unnatural; and it may even be difficult at times to grasp the sense. The *S.P.C.K. Psalter* indicates the words to be "dwelt upon" by open spacing the letters of that word as in (*d*).

(*d*) *S.P.C.K. Psalter*

O Lord h e a l me ǀ for my | bones are | vexed

(Psalm 6:2)

Words to be lightened and hurried over slightly are marked with a dot underneath. This method (*e*) is adopted by several psalters.

(*e*) *S.P.C.K. Psalter*　　　　To Thee all Angels | cry ạ | loud

(Te Deum)

SOME VERSES ARE TOO SHORT TO BE POINTED NATURALLY

This can be seen in the example (*a*) from the *New Cathedral Psalter*; the problem has generally been solved by running two verses together, as shown in (*b*).

(*a*) *New Cathedral Psalter*

Thou art the | King of | Glory: O̊ | – | – | Christ

Thou art the ev-er- | lasting | Son: of | – the | Fa- | ther

(*b*) *Worcester Psalter*

Thou art the King of | Glory. O | Christ:

Thou art the ever- | lasting | Son. of the | Father

(Te Deum)

The *Oxford Psalter* indicates this by enclosing the verse number in brackets (6) — this means, go straight on to the next line without stopping. The *S.P.C.K. Psalter* uses (+) = obelus. To indicate the position of the bar-lines, but to show that they have no effect, two half bar-lines '' are used, as shown in the example (*c*).

(*c*) + For | He hath. **re** | garded ‖ the lowli | ness of | his hand | maiden

(Te Deum)

SYLLABLES MAY RUN IN GROUPS OF THREE OR FOUR (OR MORE)

That is to say — one strong syllable followed by two or three weak ones. The 4 above the word "low" in example (*c*) above indicates the position of a stressed syllable followed by three weak syllables.

THE COMMA, WITHOUT A BREATH

A reader may take a breath at a comma, or again he may not. Where he would probably not take a breath, though he would make a momentary hesitation, the psalters usually give an extra space in the set-out of the print, as in the example given below.

Worcester Psalter

And I said 　'O that I had | wings. like a | dove

(Psalm 55:6)

SECOND HALF OF CHANT

The second half of the chant may be needed when there is an odd number of verses, or to close a section of a psalm. This is indicated by different signs in the different psalters (*S.P.C.K.* = *; *Oxford* = 2nd part; *Worcester* = +). If the particular verse is very short, the last quarter of the chant (i.e. the last six notes) only may be used. This is indicated by "half" (*S.P.C.K.*) or "last phrase" (*Oxford*). An example is given below.

S.P.C.K.

half　　W h o s o doeth t h c s e | things shall | never | fall.

cf. *Worcester Psalter*　　+ Whoso | doeth. these | things:

Shall | ne -| ver | fall

(Psalm 15:7)

REFRAINS OR REPEATED VERSES

These are often marked in italics (as in the example from the *Worcester Psalter* given below) and can be treated differently— either Full or Unison.

Worcester Psalter　　*For His* | *mercy. en-* | *dureth. for* | *ever*

(Psalm 136)

These "methods", by which the singing of psalms is made more natural, will all assist a choir to chant better. But the success of the whole thing really depends on the choirmaster—if he has a clear perception of how the music should be sung, he can make almost any choir do it, by almost any method. A good reader is potentially a good singer of psalms—and it is amazing how few good readers there are, as one soon discovers when looking for lesson-readers in the service of Nine Lessons and Carols. Therefore methods *are* necessary to help people to sing naturally, but the methods are only aids towards what is essentially a natural skill.

The Church of England has recently published an official *Revised Psalter*. Choirmasters may find it interesting to compare the improvements in this psalter against their own.

Some organists are very adamant about certain chants being suited to certain psalms. Perhaps a "penitential psalm" is best suited to a chant in a minor key—but on the whole chants have been deliberately constructed so that they are relatively smooth and characterless; the harmonies are mainly conventional. In this way a congregation or choir can learn the tunes quickly, and can then give its mind to good pointing and eventually good sense.

Should a congregation have pointed psalters? This is obviously an ideal—but a pointed psalter without a little tactful help in its use will not serve much purpose.

If the congregation is expected to sing in the psalms (and why not?), new chants will need as careful introduction as new hymns; they will have to be repeated at regular intervals—once a year is not enough!

Organists occasionally write their own chants. There certainly is a need for chants with a different sound. The commonplace harmonies and tunes (though they have served a purpose) are very tedious to the ears of a real musician; they are nearly all products of the Victorian era, and obey very uninspired academic rules of harmony. The harmony might well be more adventurous. Need chants always be in four parts, and need the form always be R 2B E–R 4B E?

There have been attempts to vary the form of the chant. "Troyte No. 1", "Troyte No. 2", etc., in the hymn books. The repetitive *Benedicite*, with its three-verse sections, has had some chant-settings with the chant in slightly different forms.

The *Gélineau Psalms*, which are frequently used in the Roman Catholic Church, and to some extent in other Churches, represent another successful method of setting prose to music. They are published by *The Grail*, and are not expensive. The tunes used are often adapted Hebrew melodies, and these are the elastic framework (as with Anglican chants) for the words. Many of the psalms have little refrains (often in 6/8 time), and these may have choral settings (SATB). They have a different flavour, and this is refreshing. Two examples follow.

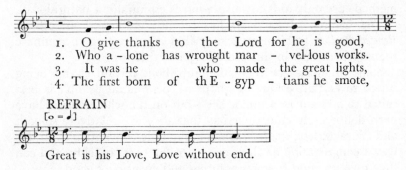

1. O give thanks to the Lord for he is good,
2. Who a - lone has wrought mar - vel-lous works.
3. It was he who made the great lights,
4. The first born of th E - gyp - tians he smote,

REFRAIN
[o = ♩]

Great is his Love, Love without end.

The short excerpt above gives the first third of the first four verses. There is a regular pulse, unlike the Anglican chant, and the words have to be fitted to this beat, sometimes faster, sometimes slower — the aim of naturalness will be the same, the method of achieving it slightly different. The choir (SATB) sings humming chords during the verse part, and bursts in with the words at the refrain "Great is His Love"; the choral setting, which is slightly contrapuntal and illustrates the less conventional harmony, has been omitted here for lack of space.

FERIAL TONE. CANTICLE OF OUR LADY (MAGNIFICAT)*

(Mode: Lah; Tonic: G)

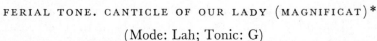

1. My soul glorifies the Lord
2. He looks on his servant in her nothingness:

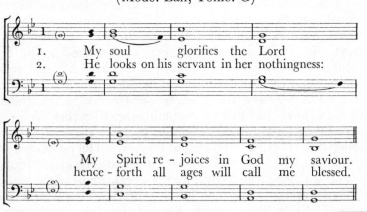

My Spirit re - joices in God my saviour.
hence - forth all ages will call me blessed.

* By kind permission of *The Grail* (England)

For verses 3–8 the last half of the tune is slightly shortened and the harmonies are a little different; verses 9 and 10 return to the tune as above. There is also an *antiphon** at the foot of the page, which is in a regular 2/4 rhythm; $\downarrow$ of the antiphon $= \circ$ of the canticle. It is not made clear how often the antiphon is to be sung.

An even simpler method of singing prose to music is to *intone* it, on one note. The same principles—no hurry, clear articulation, make good sense of the words, keep together, stress certain words, lighten others, group the syllables in twos, threes, fours, etc., apply, as with other psalms. There are two other problems:

PICKING UP THE INITIAL NOTE

Some ministers have great difficulty in picking up the first note. Provided this has not become an ingrained habit or a complex, an organist should try to find time to help the sufferer. This is really a big problem—it means either a bad listener or an inability to make the vocal cords respond to what the ear hears—but both problems can be overcome with time and patience. Surely, this is a very important matter: it irritates congregation, choir, organist—everything possible should be done to overcome this difficulty. Here are a few suggestions (we will assume that this is a new assistant minister).

(1) The minister has not done enough *listening*. He should find time to come to part or the whole of the choir practice each week.

(2) He is probably "placing" his voice wrongly. The organist should help him to sense the voice "in the mask"—that is, resonating in the cheeks. The sound can be sensed initially in the roof of the mouth—*not* in the throat. Humming can help a lot.

(3) The organist may not be using the easiest stop from which to pick up the note. Let the organist get the help of a friend, put himself in the minister's pew, and try the minister's job with different stops.

(4) As the note is given, let the minister shut his eyes (momentarily) so that he uses his ears (astonishing how many people detract from their listening ability by looking at something at the same time—listening is one thing, looking another) and try to hum with the organ note. *Place* this hum so that the sides of the nose vibrate (this can be felt); if the sound is nasal, this is because

* *Antiphon:* alternate or responsive singing between two sections of a choir, or between a single voice and the congregation.

the nostrils are being blocked off; leave the passages free—sniff out, before humming.

(5) To sing the same note as one has just hummed may present difficulty. Change the hum very slowly to an EE. These two sounds are very similar. Now to other vowels—and then to words.

KEEPING ON THE SAME NOTE

If either minister or choir is very bad at this, the organist should help. If there is a tendency to go flat, add a 4' stop—if there is a tendency to go sharp (unusual) add a 16' stop. The secret of good intonation is good listening. To make the choir listen better at practices, one can hum before each phrase. This makes the choir more aware of variations in pitch (e.g. *Hum* G, sing "Our Father". *Hum* G, sing "Which art in heaven". *Hum* G, etc. Is the G exactly the same?). The organist should have signs by which he can indicate to the choir "You are going flat—or sharp"; these signs should ideally be given almost before the sharpness or flatness has occurred. This means a very alert organist!

RESPONSES

Most Anglican churches use the "Ferial" (or ordinary day-by-day) responses by Tallis. There are two sets of responses, one near the opening of Mattins and Evensong after the Lord's Prayer, and one later, after the Creed, which may be spoken or intoned. There is also the Litany which may be used from time to time. For special festivals, choirs often use the "Festal" responses.

Some choirmasters prefer to use a different set of responses altogether. There are the alternative unison responses to be found in *The Oxford Psalter* (O.U.P.); there is *Four Settings of the Preces and Responses by Tudor Composers*, edited by Atkins and Fellowes (O.U.P., for Church Music Society)—this also includes a four-part setting by William Smith, edited by Richard Graves. Most of the great Tudor composers have set the responses to music in different ways. A new set of responses needs sympathetic introduction; the minister should warn the congregation that some new music is being tried out—possibly a short practice should take place before the service; if four weeks' warning even precedes this congregational practice, it will be found that there are very few objections. Secondly, the choir should know the new

46

music very well, and make it sound good. Thirdly, it should be practised *with* the minister. If the responses do not go too well, and the usual inevitable objections come up, bury them for a year, making a private resolve to practise them more thoroughly next time!

Nowadays, amens are rarely sung after hymns. An ancient rule was to sing amen after the last verse if it contained a doxology; this rule is retained in *The English Hymnal*. If amens are to be sung (and in one or two cases they are possibly better included — such as at the end of verse 4 of Parry's "O praise ye the Lord"), warning should be given. The main places for amens are (1) after intoned prayers, and (2) at the end of the service after the blessing.

AFTER INTONED PRAYERS

If the intonation note varies — it might be placed very low to suit a particular minister, or it might go down to E for the second Lord's Prayer — the four-part standard Plagal Amen may be too low. It is probably better then for the organist to give the choir a sign — "sing the amen in unison". Some suitable hand movement can achieve this. A different handsign can then indicate that the next amen is to be in four parts (keep off four-part unaccompanied singing if the altos are all away on holiday!). Some liturgical experts prefer a unison amen, to a unison prayer.

With the Festal Responses there are three different amens. The organist can help here by indicating One, Two, Three. If by any chance there is a fourth prayer, the organist can save the situation by indicating which of the amens is to be repeated.

AT THE END OF THE SERVICE

Most hymn books have a small section of amens, in addition to the "Dresden" and "Sevenfold". There are, of course, many huge amens from the great works which might be used for very special occasions (with the approval of the minister), and the organist might surely be allowed to write his own amen for after the blessing. A spoken blessing can also be concluded very effectively with a spoken amen.

CHAPTER THREE

VERSE SET TO MUSIC

Hymns occupy a strong position in the affections of most adherents of the Church of England and the Free Churches. "I do hope you can come and play a few hymns," says the minister to the organist, when discussing some extra service, "it will make such a difference to the service." Hymns add a sort of life-blood, an emotional warmth to the ceremonial, and there is therefore a great deal of discussion about what constitutes a good (or bad) hymn. There are, of course, many types of hymns.

PLAINSONG HYMNS

Possibly the oldest, even pre-Christian in origin. (A few of these hymns have achieved popularity among non-Catholics — "Come Holy Ghost, our souls inspire" is among the best known — possibly as plainsong has a restricted sense of rhythm.) These hymns should be sung with a strong sense of *pulse*, however, the syllables falling usually into groups of two or three (occasionally four, five or even six syllables occur before another stress is encountered), but basically each syllable is equal in duration to the next. At the end of a line, time is allowed for the taking of a breath — but the breath is to be taken quickly so that the flow of *legato* melody is not unduly interrupted. The music is not supposed to rise to great climaxes, nor should it be over-accompanied. There are some models of accompaniment by J. H. Arnold in *The English Hymnal*, which contains a large number of plainsong hymns. The dotted rhythms appearing at the end of lines in some hymn books are an editorial addition, and are out of style; they should be omitted — smoothed out to equal notes. A good organist should try to introduce one or two plainsong hymns in the course of a year; the melodies are often of a very beautiful shape (rise and fall), and their unemotional character is ideally suited to a more reflective type of religion, which has its place in the scheme of things. Though it may be more "correct" to sing a plainsong hymn rather gently with a light accompaniment, it may be found in experience that the congregation stops singing and develops an inferiority complex in the face of the choir. A just balance must be found between what is correct and what is effective. If your hymn book contains a plainsong hymn* written as shown in (a) below it is better to rewrite it mentally, as in (b).

(a)

Come Ho - ly   Ghost, our souls in - spire

The clear visual impression (no bar-lines, grouping of quavers, no long note at the end) will radically alter the way in which the hymn is sung.

FOUR-SQUARE TYPE HYMNS

Hymn tunes like *Dundee, Franconia, St. Flavian, Old Hundredth* are usually good congregational hymns, as the rhythmic side is very simple. The first note of some of these tunes (e.g. *Old Hundredth*) is sometimes written with two beats, sometimes with one beat. The purpose of the two beats was to give the congregation extra time to catch up: the organist needs to make up his mind whether he is to give one or two beats, and then to keep to this scheme; in this way a tradition is built up. Two beats may also give a hymn a little more rhythmic interest. On the other hand it may be found more difficult to make the breath last out, particularly if the pace is slow. Some churches have been experimenting with singing these four-square hymns quite fast, thus producing a lighter effect. An ancient hymn need not necessarily be sung slowly; there are arguments on all sides.

A choir should be very determined to avoid the "plod-plod" effect which these hymns tend to produce. Each line should be treated as a unit or phrase with one or two natural stresses chosen from the sense of the words.

* This is not authentic plainsong, but the result of an attempt (in the nineteenth century in Mechlin, Belgium) to revive plainsong hymn tunes in a form which would appeal to those unfamiliar with plainsong proper.

Tunes like *Jerusalem, Repton, Austrian Hymn, Hyfrydol, Nun Danket*, etc., where the music rises to a strong climax and the congregation can be expected to take the top notes with a healthy roar, often give a service a good start or finish; a unison hymn is of course better for a procession. (A list of 100 Stirring Tunes will be found in Appendix Three.)

The sense of phrase is here, as ever, important. The "top-note" itself needs to be part of the contour, not an isolated mountain peak; and the choir should know where to take breaths, and what to do with long notes.

HYMNS WITH PRONOUNCED RHYTHM

These are usually "strong" tunes as well, but not necessarily broad ones. *Truro*, "I Love To Hear The Story", *Hilariter, Morning Light, Marching, Quittez, Pasteurs*, are some examples. The rhythm must be good. It is relatively easy to play ♩ ♫ ♩ , but not so easy to sing "Je-sus shall reign", bringing the "shall" and "reign" very close together; then getting the choir unanimous, and finally incorporating the good rhythm into the overall phrase.

CONTEMPLATIVE HYMNS

Many chorale-tunes come under this heading; e.g. *Passion Chorale, Schmücke dich.* Other hymns may have a lazy lilting rhythm (especially in triple time), e.g. *Surrey, St. Columba, Wareham*. These tunes are usually sung *legato* without too much difficulty. Rhythmically they may tend to "go to sleep", and this will need counteracting at the practice.

These are some of the hymn-types as regards the melody; many hymns come partly under one heading and partly under another. When selecting hymns for a service, there should not be too many of any one type. The question of key also needs watching; not too many hymns in any one key. Some hymn books have very useful indexes to help in the matter of selection; especially the recent *Anglican Hymn Book*.

How to rehearse and practise hymns is treated separately in Chapter Six.

To introduce a new hymn book into a church is an expensive business; one must be absolutely sure it is worth doing. Although hymn books differ considerably, a choirmaster can usually make a selection of the hymns he thinks good, discarding the rest, and this should provide enough material. Musical, theological and literary tastes, however, are always on the move, and there may come a time when a minister, or an organist, or a congregation wants a change. The words of hymns—let us face it—are still pretty poor stuff as poetry, or even as natural everyday speech.

> "Who is this with garments gory,
> Triumphing from Bozrah's way;"
> (A. C. Coxe, 1818–1896; *E.H.*, No. 108)

> "His are the thousand sparkling rills
> That from a thousand fountains burst,
> And fill with music all the hills;
> And yet He saith, 'I thirst'."
> (Mrs. C. F. Alexander, 1823–1895; *E.H.* No. 117; *Ch.H.*,
> No. 101; *A. & M.* (Rev.), No. 120)

But these words are often attached to, and inseparable from, quite good tunes. And, further, there are not too many hymns suitable for occasions like, say, Maundy Thursday. There is surely an opportunity for men of taste and literary ability and faith to produce something better. Non-Christians find this sort of stuff pretty poor, and use it as one of their reasons for their lack of interest in the Church. Some words, however, are too individual (even though of high quality) to be sung by a congregation. When, in addition, the sense goes across the line, the result as sung (with breaths in the wrong places) can become, to say the least, unconvincing.

> "Strong is the lion, like a coal (*wrong breath*)
> His eyeball, like a bastion's mole (*wrong breath*)
> His chest against the foes:
> Strong the gier-eagle on his sail;" etc.
> (Christopher Smart, 1722–1771, *S. of P.*, No. 690)

> "Yet gifts should prove their use:
> I own the Past profuse
> Of power each side, perfection every turn:

51

Eyes, ears took in their dole,
Brain treasured up the whole;
Should not the heart beat once: 'How good to
    live and learn'!"
(Robert Browning, 1812–1889, *S. of P.*, No. 662).

As poetry these last two are superb in their thought-content, imagery and quality of words, but as hymns . . .

THE "MORALITY" HYMN

Some hymn writers for the young have produced "goody-goody" hymns. "Christian children all must be Mild, obedient, good as He". This twisting of Christianity to back one's own system of morality, to "keep the children quiet", has produced some fairly bad hymns.

What in fact makes a good hymn?* Simple direct emotions, perhaps, avoiding obscurities and difficult language; the words fitting a metre in fairly regular form; no bombast, insincerity, purple passages; a real idea working through the verses. The writer must be first a poet, secondly a Christian,† ideally a Christian poet.

After this fairly full discussion of hymn tunes and words, let us look at some of the available hymn books (see also Appendix Two).

CHURCH OF ENGLAND

Hymns Ancient and Modern, Standard Edition (Clowes, 1861: with first supplement 1889, and second supplement 1916). Perhaps the commonest of Church of England hymn books, but as new hymns were added in the form of supplements this produced:

Hymns Ancient and Modern, Revised Edition (Clowes, 1950). This is one of the best hymn books, with clear large type (in the Organ Edition), plainsong hymns in quavers without bar-lines, an abundance of Victorian favourites, a reasonable selection of Tudor hymns, words good and bad, rather a heavy proportion of four-square hymns, missionary hymns have been pruned, descants

---

* There is some interesting, though not entirely convincing, discussion on this in *Praises with Understanding* by Horace Spence (R.S.C.M.).

† To many this may seem to be the wrong way round. Then look up some of the hymns written by the Revd. X and Bishop Y.

sound but not often inspiring. In both the Standard and Revised Editions, a Transposed Tune Book is published, with every tune in a lower key (without words); this is especially useful for unison singing.

Songs of Praise (O.U.P., 1926, enlarged 1932). Another good book, type clear (though not as clear as in the larger editions of *A. & M.* (Rev.)), plainsong hymns, alas, in minims with bar-lines, not so many Victorian old favourites, plenty of Tudor hymns, some superb descants (especially by Vaughan Williams), many hymns and descants by Martin and Geoffrey Shaw, a great many folk tunes replacing the four-square tune abundance in *A. & M.* Some complaints about excessive admiration of nature come from orthodox circles, and one or two of the experiments with "strong" poetry would need a sermon or two, before the whole congregation could understand what they were singing about. A greater number of truly "musical" flowing tunes than in *A. & M.* (Rev.). Altogether a more cultured book than *A. & M.* (Rev.), though not necessarily a better one.

The English Hymnal (O.U.P. and A. R. Mowbray, 1906, revised 1933). Another good hymn book, type rather small and paper not very good. This is the specialist hymn book for those who like plainsong hymns, and is used in many churches with a liturgical tradition. The words of the plainsong hymns, when translated from Latin into rhymed verse, sometimes verge on the side of doggerel, but the theology is to the point, if a little monastic. Owing to a great deal of space taken up by the plainsong side there is less room for old favourites, though a good many are still to be found. The first pruning of poorer Victorian hymns was obviously a little too severe, and an appendix was added in which some of the "musts" have re-appeared.

The English Hymnal Service Book (O.U.P., 1962). This contains, in addition to 298 hymns from *The English Hymnal*, a supplement of 37 hymns and carols from other sources, the Psalter (simply pointed), Merbecke's setting of the Holy Communion, the Ferial Responses, etc. The book is designed to help the congregation "to unite in the truly corporate use of the Prayer Book services of Mattins, Holy Communion and Evensong". Like *The English Hymnal*, the *Service Book* contains lists of suitable hymns for all seasons of the Christian Year.

Anglican Hymn Book (Church Book Room Press, 1965). A new book, successor to the *Hymnal Companion to the Book of Common Prayer*, and *The Church Hymnal for the Christian Year*. A special feature is the superb 62-page index. There is a theme-index for each hymn tune, a scripture passage reference so that hymns can be found to suit a given text, lists of alternative hymns for occasions, all in clear large type. The choice of hymn tunes is wide; old favourites are there if needed, but there is usually a second tune if the old favourite is of doubtful quality. Some exciting choral arrangements are included (e.g. D. Willcox) for ambitious choirs. The descants are more original than in other books; the rhythm is occasionally tricky. There are new tunes, one or two harmonically adventurous (e.g. No. 5). Not all the hymns with poor words have been thrown out. Plainsong hymns are written in quavers. The Christmas selection of hymns is remarkably good — about twenty congregational favourites and other interesting hymns are included.

The English Catholic Hymn-Book (W. Knott & Sons). A small hymn book intended for Anglo-Catholic churches; it does not seem to be in frequent use. There is no music edition, tunes from existing tune books being suggested for each hymn.

Hymnal for Scotland (O.U.P.). This is *The English Hymnal* to which some hymns of Scottish interest have been added, mainly in connection with Scottish saints. In 1950 it was authorised for use in the Episcopal Church of Scotland, which is a province of the Anglican Church.

ROMAN CATHOLIC

The Westminster Hymnal (Burns & Oates, 1912, revised 1940 and 1946). The 1912 edition, the first authorised Roman Catholic hymnal in this country, was musically edited by Sir Richard Terry. The 1940 revision, edited by Dom Gregory Murray, though a considerable improvement on the earlier edition, met with no great success with Roman Catholic congregations. Now that hymn singing is becoming more popular in Roman Catholic churches, the 1964 revised edition, edited by the Revd. W. S. Bainbridge, may be received with more enthusiasm. It contains some 275 English and Latin hymns, and an appendix of alternative tunes to 16 hymns. There are many tunes from the old German hymnaries, and from the French Catholic church melodies in which old plainsong tunes were transformed into measured hymn tunes.* The melodies in the Latin section are mostly taken from Gregorian chant.

The Leeds Catholic Hymnal (Catholic Printing Co. of Farnworth, 1954). This hymnal was compiled by Cardinal Heenan when he was Bishop of Leeds. There are 108 English and Latin hymns and anthems (some of which are taken from *The Westminster Hymnal*), as well as the complete Benediction and Novena to Our Lady.

The Catholic Hymn Book (Catholic Printing Co. of Farnworth, 1954). Compiled by the clergy of Salford Cathedral for parochial and school use, this is a smaller hymn book than the above, though many of the 61 hymns are to be found in both books.

The whole question of metrical hymn singing amongst English Roman Catholics during the Mass has now changed; it is expected that a new Roman Catholic hymnal will soon be published.

BAPTIST

The Baptist Hymn Book (Carey Kingsgate Press Ltd., for Psalms and Hymns Trust, 1962). This replaces *The Baptist Hymnal* (1900, revised 1933) from which about two-thirds of the hymns have been retained. Of the 850 or so hymns and chants, 36 are by Charles Wesley and 26 by Isaac Watts; more than 300 are common to other hymn books. Along with hymns of *The English Hymnal* type are many of the "Sankey" variety; and this is the first hymn book to include two of the Beaumont hymns from the *Twentieth Century Folk Mass*; No. 18 ("Now thank we all our God") and No. 250 ("Lord, Thy word abideth").

CONGREGATIONAL

Congregational Praise (Independent Press, 1951). This was published in succession to the *Congregational Hymnary* (1916). The choice of tunes is similar to *A. & M.*; the words, however, are different. Isaac Watts and Charles Wesley between them are responsible for the words of nearly 100 of the 778 hymns, and the commonest composers are J. S. Bach, Barnby, Dykes, Smart, Thiman; and there is a selection of metrical psalms from the

* Many of the French church melodies are included in *The English Hymnal* and in most hymn books of all denominations. See the Revd. C. E. Pocknee's *The French Diocesan Hymns and their Melodies* (Faith Press).

Scottish Psalter. The hymn book ends with a selection of psalms (some abridged) and passages from scripture for chanting.

METHODIST

The Methodist Hymn Book (Epworth Press, 1933). It is worth quoting a small passage from the introduction to *A Collection of Hymns for use of the people called Methodists* by John Wesley (1779). "(1) In these hymns there is no doggerel; no botches; nothing put in to patch up the rhyme; no feeble expletives. (2) Here is nothing turgid or bombast, on the one hand, or low and creeping on the other. (3) Here are no *cant* expressions, no words without meaning. Those who impute this to us know not what they say. We talk common sense, both in prose and verse, and use no word but in a fixed and determinate sense. (4) Here are, allow me to say, both the purity, the strength, and the elegance of the English language; and, at the same time, the utmost simplicity and plainness, suited to every capacity. Lastly, I desire men of taste to judge (these are the only competent judges), whether there be not in some of the following hymns the true Spirit of Poetry, such as cannot be acquired by art and labour, but must be the gift, of nature." A bold claim for any hymn book! Since Wesley's day, a great many hymns from all sources have been added, so the best tunes common to all hymn books are here; the hymn tunes peculiar to this book tend to be bright and cheerful, rather simple, and direct in form. There is a selection of canticles and psalms, and passages from Scripture set to music, at the end of the book. This is one of the largest hymn books; nearly one thousand hymns. It is sometimes used by churches of other denominations (e.g. Baptist).

PRESBYTERIAN

The Church Hymnary (O.U.P., revised edition, 1927). Authorised for use by the Church of Scotland, the United Free Church of Scotland, the Presbyterian Church of Scotland, Ireland, England, Wales, etc. A very good hymn book. In addition to an excellent collection of hymns under the general headings: God, His Being, Works, and Word; The Church; The Christian Life; Times and Seasons; Travellers and the Absent; National Hymns; Home and

School; Mission Services; Doxologies; and Ancient Hymns and Canticles, there is a supplement for the Presbyterian Church of England and Wales—this contains metrical psalms, prose psalms and canticles, and Scripture sentences. A further revised edition is expected shortly.

THE SALVATION ARMY

The Song Book of the Salvation Army (Salvationist Publishing and Supplies). Contains 983 songs (i.e. hymns), benedictions and choruses. *The Salvation Army Tune Book* (with supplement, 1953), which provides the music for *The Song Book*, is arranged for voices and organ, or piano, and is a companion to the *Band Tune Book*. Many of the songs are composed by Salvation Army Officers and Soldiers: in some the words are fitted to well-known tunes such as *Annie Laurie, Genevieve, Home Sweet Home* and *Poor Old Joe* (but this type of tune is not used so much nowadays); there are also many standard popular hymn tunes such as *Ravenshaw, Richmond, Old Hundredth, Duke Street*, etc. A second supplement (1963) adds a further 51 tunes to the *Tune Book*.

OTHER FREE CHURCHES

The Liturgy and Hymns Authorized for use in The Moravian Church in Great Britain and Ireland (revised edition, 1912, with supplements, 1937 and 1938, Moravian Church House, 5–7 Muswell Hill, London, N.10). This hymn book for the British Province of the Moravian Church (which has some forty churches in this country) contains 952 hymns, in addition to The Liturgy, the Canticles, etc. There are some fine German hymns with English translations, as well as many standard hymns (with a wide selection of tunes by S. S. Wesley).

Redemption Hymnal (1951, revised 1955, Elim Publishing House). This is the usual hymn book used by the churches in the British Pentecostal Fellowship, comprising over a thousand churches in this country. It is published by a hymnal committee on which each of the three main pentecostal groups are represented; Assemblies of God, The Elim Church, and the Apostolic Church. A special aim is to provide an adequate number of hymns whose emphasis is upon the "baptism in the Holy Spirit". The 800 hymns include many devotional and revival hymns, some psalms in metrical paraphrase, and a very few hymns for children. Some of the standard tunes are set to new words by Pentecostal writers, and there are quite a few of the verse-refrain type, by Sankey, William Booth, and kindred writers; also a few tunes by Vaughan Williams (*Randolph*), Martin Shaw (*Marching*), etc.

INTERDENOMINATIONAL AND MISSION HYMN BOOKS, ETC.

The Cambridge Hymnal, edited by David Holbrook and Elizabeth Poston (Cambridge University Press, 1967). A new collection of nearly 200 hymns, carols, and anthems for schools, colleges churches, etc. Ths is a hymnal expressive of Christian thought and feeling in the twentieth century; apart from familiar words and music there are hymns with new words (including some by modern poets), and new settings by composers such as Britten, Berkeley, Copland, Rubbra, and Stravinsky. Included are Negro spirituals, primitive American hymns, and an African chant, and there is a good variety of descant.

The B.B.C. Hymn Book (O.U.P., 1951). Musically edited by Dr. Stanton, Dr. Thalben-Ball, and the Revd. Cyril Taylor, this has a section of metrical psalms and Bible paraphrases and, towards the end of the book, a number of "choir-settings" (slightly more difficult hymns and easy anthems). There are no descants, and the tunes are relatively straightforward; owing to the inter-denominational character of the book, each individual from a particular church may find a number of hymns he does not know. A book like this, however, might be very useful in the present ecumenical drive for church unity.

Hymns of Faith (Scripture Union and C.S.S.M., 1964). An all-purpose hymn book of 659 hymns, with a varied selection of hymns for special festivals—particularly Christmas.

The Golden Hymnal (Scripture Union and C.S.S.M., first published in 1890). A selection of 738 hymns for mission services, etc., also published as *Golden Bells Hymn Book*, the latter title being considered more suitable for children.

Christian Praise (Tyndale Press). An excellent interdenominational hymn book containing some 400 hymns and carols. There are a number of descants and fa-burden arrangements, and the carol section contains some simple choir settings of well-known tunes. Many modern tunes are included as alternatives to some of the older settings. This book is used by some churches, as well as by schools.

The Mirfield Mission Hymn Book (Mowbray, 1907, new edition 1948). A popular Anglo-Catholic hymn book, but used as a supplement to other hymn books in ordinary parochial worship. Two hundred and twenty hymns, early and modern, by writers from Sankey to Vaughan Williams, etc.

Songs of Syon (Schott, 1904, 1910, 1923). A collection of psalms, hymns and spiritual songs, edited by the Revd. G. R. Woodward, who himself composed many of the 431 hymns. A good deal of the music in *E.H.* is the result of Woodward's researches. A few of Woodward's hymns appear in modern hymn books(e.g. *Cong. P.* Nos. 712, 719, 726). Charles Wood contributed some fine settings to this collection.

Redemption Songs (Pickering & Inglis). One thousand hymns and choruses for evangelistic meetings, etc.

Believers Hymn Book (Pickering & Inglis). Three hundred and sixty select scriptural hymns with 103 additional hymns added as a supplement; suitable for mission services, etc.

Keswick Hymn-Book (Marshall, Morgan & Scott). A revision (1936) of *Hymns of Consecration and Faith*, which for many years was used at the Keswick Convention, and other gatherings of a similar character, for the "deepening of spiritual life". Among the 558 hymns, doxologies, etc., there are tunes by Sankey, tunes of the verse-refrain type, and (like *The Salvation Army Tune Book*) some of the words are set to traditional melodies (e.g. Nos. 356 *Ar Hyd Y Nos*, 357 *Prospect*, 493 *Forest Green*). There is also a good mixture of old and modern tunes, including some by Vaughan Williams, Martin Shaw, etc.

The Fellowship Hymnbook (1909, revised 1933, published for the National Adult School Union and the Brotherhood Movement Incorporated, by Novello and George Allen & Unwin). It is used by senior schools and colleges and, on occasions, by the Religious Society of Friends for evening meetings (not for their services, which have no music). There are some 420 hymns, including modern ones by Walford Davies, Martin Shaw, Vaughan Williams, etc.

We may note in passing that several hymn books (e.g. *Hymns Ancient and Modern*, *The (Revised) Church Hymnary*, *The Methodist*

59

Hymn Book, *Congregational Praise*, *Redemption Songs*) are published in Tonic Solfa editions; and that the words of many are available in Braille (a list of these can be obtained from The National Institute for the Blind, 224 Great Portland Street, London, W.1). Organ editions of a few hymn books are published, with larger music type and words than in the ordinary music editions; *Hymns Ancient and Modern* (Standard), *The (Revised) Church Hymnary*, and *The Methodist Hymn Book*. The Organ edition of *Hymns Ancient and Modern* (revised) is considerably smaller than the first three.

SCHOOL AND SUNDAY SCHOOL HYMN BOOKS

Of the many "school" hymn books some are shortened versions of hymn books already described; others are specially compiled. Certain hymn books, such as *Songs of Praise*, *The English Hymnal*, and *The English Hymnal Service Book* are used in schools as well as churches.

Hymns Ancient and Modern (Clowes). A School edition (with Daily Services) was published in 1958.

Songs of Praise (O.U.P.). There are several school hymn books based on this: (1) *Songs of Praise for Boys and Girls* (1930), 113 hymns and carols suitable for all ages; (2) *Hymns for use in Schools*, and *Hymns for use in Junior Schools*, useful senior and junior abridgements of *Songs of Praise*; (3) *The Daily Service* (1936, revised 1947), services for all ages, together with 172 hymns and carols from *Songs of Praise*; also similar Service Books with added supplements for London, Northern Ireland, and Wales.

Hymns for Church and School (Nov., 1964). This is the fourth edition of *The Public School Hymnbook*, and is edited by a Committee appointed by the Headmasters' Conference in 1960. This book, containing 346 hymns (some new, many excellent, a few indifferent), is intended to bridge the gap between school and church.

The Clarendon Hymn Book (O.U.P., 1936), with 300 hymns (16 in Latin) suitable for schools and colleges; published originally for Charterhouse, it contains some good modern-style hymns.

A Student's Hymnal (O.U.P., 1923), for use in schools and colleges, with 206 English hymns, 123 Welsh hymns, and some psalms, anthems and carols.

Hymns of the Kingdom (O.U.P.), the English hymns from the above.

Scottish School Hymnary (O.U.P., 1964), the first school hymn book for primary school children (aged seven to twelve) in Scotland; compiled by the Church Hymnary Trust and the Scottish Joint Committee on Religious Education, mainly from *The Revised Church Hymnary*.

Children Praising (O.U.P., 1937). With 102 short hymns, lullabies, etc., for children up to six years old, edited by Herbert Wiseman and W. H. Hamilton, and sponsored by the Committee on the Religious Instruction of Youth in the Church of Scotland.

Church and School Hymnal (S.P.C.K., 1926). An excellent collection of 338 hymns, carols, etc., for the young, including some for the very young.

The English School Hymn Book, edited by Desmond Macmahon (University of London Press, 1939). The 207 hymns, canticles, and psalms, etc., include fourteen French hymns and thirty Christmas hymns and carols. The idea expressed in the words of the poetry is mainly one of joy and thanksgiving; the tunes have rhythmic and melodic interest, and many have been transposed to bring them into the upper range of the child's voice.

Catholic Schools Assembly Book, compiled by the Revd. F. H. Drinkwater (University of London Press, 1961, 2nd edition 1965). 141 hymns, the tunes of which are to be found in *The Westminster Hymnal* (Old and New) and other hymn books; also some psalms, benedictions, etc., and a Liturgical Supplement.

Hymns for Catholic Schools (Burns & Oates). Compiled by the (Roman) Catholic Teachers' Federation.

The Methodist School Hymn Book (Epworth Press, 1914, revised 1950).

Hymns in Harmony (B. & H.), devised by Dorothy Hogben for use in girls' schools, for S.S.A. and piano.

School Worship (Thalben-Ball) and *A Book of Worship for Youth*, published in 1926 by the Independent Press (Congregational) and the Psalms and Hymns Trust (Baptist); these books, though containing many good tunes, do not seem to have been widely adopted.

The Young People's Song Book of The Salvation Army (Salvationist Publishing and Supplies, 1963) contains 395 songs and benedictions, many of them taken from *The Salvation Army Tune Book*.

Sunday School Praise (National Sunday School Union, 1958), 583 hymns, responsive services, choric Bible readings and prayers.

Sunday School Hymnary (1905) and *Child Songs* (1908), also published by the National Sunday School Union.

BOOKS ABOUT HYMN BOOKS

Historical Companion to Hymns Ancient and Modern, edited by Maurice Frost (William Clowes, 1962). This revision of Bishop Frere's book of the same title, which was published in 1909, is by far the largest, most handsome and lavishly illustrated of all the Companions to hymnals; it is also the most costly, but may be consulted at many public libraries. Detailed notes are included on the words and music of the revised edition (1950) of *Hymns Ancient and Modern*, and there are briefer notes covering all the other editions from 1860/1 onwards. The 124-page introduction traces the history of *Hymns Ancient and Modern* from its roots in the hymnody of the early Church. Among the valuable features (in addition to notes on the words and tunes) are brief biographies of authors and composers; indexes of first lines, translated Latin hymns, plainsong and allied melodies, and tunes modern and modernised; a list of publications and tunes; and a metrical index of tunes.

Songs of Praise Discussed, compiled by Percy Dearmer, with notes on the music by Archibald Jacob (O.U.P., 1933), contains detailed notes on the words and tunes of every hymn, together with biographical and historical notes on authors, composers, sources, etc.

Handbook to the Church Hymnary, edited by James Moffatt, 1930, with supplement by Millar Patrick (O.U.P., 1936). A very good handbook, at present out of print.

The Music of the Methodist Hymn-Book, by James Lightwood (Epworth Press, fourth edition revised by Francis D. Westbrook, 1955), contains the story of each *tune* with biographical notes on the composers, also indexes of tunes, etc. The companion volume, dealing with the *words*, is:

The Methodist Hymn-Book Illustrated in History and Experience, by John Telford (Epworth Press, seventh edition, 1959). This gives the origin of every hymn, and the chief facts about its author.

Companion to Congregational Praise, edited by K. L. Parry, with notes on the music by Erik Routley (Independent Press, 1953), contains, in addition to the notes on words and tunes, some interesting articles on various subjects (names of hymn tunes, gathering-notes, Bach chorales, Welsh hymn tunes, etc.), and a useful chronological list of sources cited in the musical notes.

The Baptist Hymn Book Companion, with notes on hymns, authors and translators by the editor Hugh Martin, and on tunes and composers by Eric P. Sharpe (Psalms and Hymns Trust, 1962). There are useful articles by other writers on different aspects of Baptist music.

The Music of Christian Hymnody, by Erik Routley (Independent Press, 1937), is the first complete modern history of the hymn tune in English, and also serves as a musical commentary on *The English Hymnal*, which has no companion of its own.

Hymns in Christian Worship, by Cecil Northcott (Lutterworth Press, 1964), is a critical study of the place of hymns in various Christian liturgies; it includes an examination of "rhythm" hymns and "beat" tunes.

A Companion to the School Hymn Book of the Methodist Church, by W. S. Kelynack (Epworth Press, 1950).

A Dictionary of Hymnology, edited by J. Julian (Murray, 1892, revised 1907; republished in two vols., 1957). The standard reference book for the student of hymnology.

"POP" CHURCH MUSIC

This movement began in October 1957, when a setting of portions of the Anglican Eucharist, under the title *A Twentieth Century Folk Mass* (Weinberger, recorded on LPR 201, or MG 20019), was performed at St. Augustine's, Highgate, and also televised by the B.B.C. The music was composed in a "popular" style by Father Geoffrey Beaumont, then Vicar of St. George's, Camberwell, and now a monk of the Community of the Resurrection at Mirfield, Yorkshire. The *Folk Mass*, which in the television performance was accompanied by a large modern dance orchestra, is set for cantor* and congregation; with some exceptions, each phrase of the music for the congregation is first sung by the cantor, and then repeated by the congregation. This exact repetition

* The cantor was once an important officer in a cathedral, ranking next to the dean. Nowadays, a solo singer.

enables the congregation to learn the music in the easiest possible way although, from a musical point of view, the monotony of the procedure soon becomes evident. The hymns (Paxton), in the style of a foxtrot, waltz, etc., are perhaps the more successful though, as Dr. Erik Routley points out,* the jazz element in the *Mass* has been held by many experts in the world of light music to be already out of date. This is not, in itself, an argument against this kind of music because, in the nature of things, "jazz" music is bound to be dated (as is the term itself); nevertheless, a work such as Gershwin's *Rhapsody in Blue*, though undeniably of the "twenties", may still be acceptable to many people whose appreciation of music is far from up-to-date. But if the *Folk Mass* is presented (1) as "folk" music, or (2) as Church music in contemporary style, then we may feel that the nature of the music is misconceived. The folk element is as far removed from that of, say, Martin Shaw's *Anglican Folk Mass* (Curwen) as the "pop" element is removed from the music which is currently popular with the modern teenager. Thus the *Folk Mass* is unlikely to make a strong appeal either to the "folk" enthusiast or to the "pop" addict. Most of those Christians who have enthusiastically embraced the *Folk Mass* have probably been influenced more by the evangelical possibilities than by the fitness and quality of the music.

Father Beaumont's *Folk Mass* has, however, established the light music idiom as a factor in Christian worship, and has opened the way for many similar experiments. The "Twentieth Century Church Light Music Group", an association of composers and authors which includes Father Beaumont, the Revd. Patrick Appleford, and the Revd. Canon E. C. Blake, has produced a quantity of popular Church music; the larger works include (1) *Mass of Five Melodies* by Patrick Appleford (Weinberger, recorded on Tower CLM 209), which is a setting of the Holy Communion which can be sung by the congregation without the phrases being first "taught" by the cantor; and (2) *A Festival Te Deum* by John Alldis (Weinberger, recorded on Tower CLM 202), which is a "pop" setting for cantor and congregation, the cantor singing each phrase which is then repeated by the congregation as in the *Folk Mass*; a Choirs' Edition is also published which provides for the choir to lead the congregation in unison, and to highlight certain passages in four-part harmony.

* *Church Music and Theology* (Waltham Forest Books).

Some of the most interesting of the Church light music is that by Malcolm Williamson, the talented Australian organist who composed *Vision of Christ Phoenix* (Chappell) for the consecration of Coventry Cathedral in 1962, and *Organ Symphony*, broadcast in 1963 and as yet unpublished. Malcolm Williamson's excursions into the field of light Church music include small items such as *Twelve Hymn Tunes* (Weinberger, recorded on Tower CLM 204), and *Harvest Thanksgiving* (Weinberger, recorded on Tower 206). These are really cantatas, which, though continuous, consist of a sequence of hymns for, respectively, Passiontide and Harvest Festivals. In this music we find good, broad tunes and decisive rhythms which, while not attempting to follow current "pop" trends, have sufficient individuality to appeal not only to those of limited musical taste, but also to more experienced and cultivated musicians.

A new recruit to Church light music is Leonard Bernstein, conductor of the New York Philharmonic and composer of *West Side Story* as well as serious music; the 1965 Southern Cathedrals Festival at Chichester saw the first performance of his specially commissioned setting, in popular rhythmic form, of the *Chichester Psalms* (in Hebrew).

TWENTIETH CENTURY HYMN BOOKS

Several collections of hymns in "light music" style are published by Weinberger. These include:

Thirty 20th Century Hymn Tunes: new tunes to a variety of hymns for general congregational or mission service.

More 20th Century Hymn Tunes: thirty more hymns, similar to the above.

Twenty-Seven 20th Century Hymns: a collection of new words and tunes for use at the parish communion and other services.

ACCOMPANYING HYMNS

This appears simple enough, but a good organist makes all the difference. Here are a few points:

THE PLAY-OVER

This should be in good rhythm, at the same speed at which the hymn is to be sung; it should not end with a *ritard*. There should be a definite number of beats before the choir (or congregation without choir) starts. The registration of the play-over and the first verse should be different and decisive (*mp-mf*: *mf-f*). The best and simplest way is for the organist to prepare the Swell *mp* and the Great *mf*. As he lifts his hands off the Swell at the end of the play-over, he should keep counting and start the hymn at the exact planned moment. One method is to hold the last play-over chord for two beats, lifting it off exactly on three; count the fourth beat, and begin the hymn on the fifth. The advantage of this is that the congregation hears the silence (third beat), has one beat (the fourth) on which to take a breath, and on the fifth beat it should begin. Some organists do not like this method as it puts "an extra number of beats in the bar". However, once a procedure has been decided upon (not an *absence* of procedure!) the organist should keep to it. Ideally the congregation should be treated intelligently, and the method should be explained at a congregational practice. Plainsong-songs (moving faster) and 6/8 hymns will need slightly different methods.

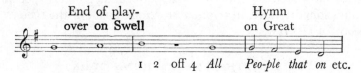

With a majestic tune (e.g. *Old Hundredth*), a first phrase can be played over *Unison* or Full Swell, without pedals—or on a tuba, trumpet or Diapason I stop (if presentable).

It is better not to play over on the Great, and then begin on the Great—it spoils the attack. But this is not an absolute rule. The play-over could be on the Great, and the hymn could begin Full Swell with pedals. The play-over could be on a single Great stop (e.g. Open Diapason I), and the addition of Swell-Great and pedals should give adequate attack. But these are points depending on taste, the individual organ, the building, the dexterity of the organist, and the relative size of choir and congregation (50 : 50 or 1 : 10!).

The point at which the play-over ends should be carefully chosen so that the last chord will *help* the congregation to begin. If a line of play-over ends with a dominant chord, and the tune starts on a tonic chord, it is best to play the whole tune or (for

66

example) lines one and four, if they can be made to fit. Even if the choir has been trained to start firmly after the dominant chord, the congregation will usually spoil it. It is also better to play the whole tune, if it is a new one which is being introduced. Again, having decided on a procedure, the organist should stick to it, so that the congregation knows what to expect when the hymn is heard again.

DIFFERENT TYPES OF HYMN NEED DIFFERENT METHODS OF ACCOMPANIMENT

(1) *Plainsong hymns* (ideal accompaniment by J. H. Arnold in *The English Hymnal*): light pedal, generally loud enough to keep the congregation singing and moving but no more; a *legato* style with a good *pulse*.

(2) *Procession* (especially if the church has an echo, or the organ speaks late, or the sound takes time to reach the end of the building): here it may be necessary to play slower, and even to emphasise the rhythm by a degree of *staccato*. Some organists keep the pulse by increasing the overall volume, or by adding to the pedal.

(3) *Four-square hymns*—which easily drag: the rhythm can be helped if the organist makes the end of each line and the start of the next absolutely clear. This can be done by lifting the hands off, one clear beat before the next line begins. As this may slightly destroy the *legato* effect also desired, a subtle way is to hold one part (or two parts), and lift the other three (or two).

Old Hundredth

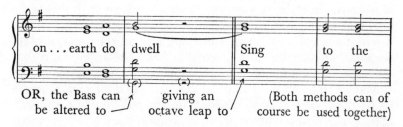

The alto achieves the *legato*, STB are lifted and give the required attack for "Sing". Any part or parts can be held across, except the soprano. Alternatively, the bass can be made to leap an octave to give definition.

67

(4) *Hymns with pronounced rhythm.* Provided that part of the organ plays *legato*, the organist should not be afraid of using some *staccato* to help the rhythm (e.g., Kocher — "O happy band of pilgrims").

TOUCH

A pianist transferring to organ usually finds it difficult to play sufficiently *legato*. In hymn-playing, repeated notes in a part other than the soprano can often be tied across. This *legato* needs constant "finger-changing" (hold G down with 2, change to 3 without letting the note up), and it is a good idea to practise downward scales played entirely with fingering 5-45-45, and upward scales 1-21-21, etc. In the play-over in particular it is easy to spot a pianist-become-organist if the *legato* is poor.

However, as soon as a *legato* foundation has been laid, it then becomes vital to "break the *legato*". The difference is that the pianist plays *non-legato* without wishing to, whilst an organist who is a discerning musician plays *non-legato* because unadulterated *legato* is so dull. *Staccato* gives variety to the phrasing, light and shade, enables the ear to disentangle the notes, and clarifies the rhythm. In a large echoey building, *staccato* is even more necessary. *Staccato* does not necessarily break a phrase.

REGISTRATION FOR ACCOMPANYING HYMNS

Different hymns need different registration. The registration depends on the ability of the choir. If the choir lacks confidence, more falls on the organist; if the choir is good, the organist can give it an unaccompanied verse (or two), even adding decorations of his own (in style, or course). With a weak choir, it would be fatal if he did so. Not all organists would agree with this, however. There is a school of thought which argues that the organist plays the same whether the choir is good or bad. The argument is that the organist plays for the congregation, not for the choir.

Many hymns have an implied rise and fall dynamically *within the verse*. *Jerusalem* (Parry) without rise and fall would be unthinkable. If this is approached gradually, one of the simpler methods is to begin the verse with Full Swell (including octave couplers), but with the box closed. As the verse proceeds the box is gradually opened. One can, of course, be playing on the Great, with the Swell-Great drawn. If the "top point" is relatively sudden (e.g.

Old Hundredth, Veni Emmanuel), it is probably better to add stops. Apart from pistons, one of the simpler ways is to add Swell-Great at the critical moment; or if the Swell-Great is already drawn, add octave couplers on the Swell.

Gradual Crescendos:	Swell Box.
	Adding stops gradually (more difficult).
Sudden Increases:	Pistons (hands or feet).
	Adding several stops together.
	Adding Swell-Great.
	Adding octave couplers.

A few suggestions for a two-manual organ are given below. If the congregation comes in sluggishly with the first note, it will probably be necessary to add at least one extra beat to that note. In time, with good rhythm and attack from both choir and organist, this can be reduced.

Old Hundredth (G Major) Four Verses

All People That On Earth Do Dwell

GOOD CHOIR	CHOIR LACKING CONFIDENCE
Prepare: Sw. or Gt. (strong stop, e.g. Trpt., Open Diap. I). Sw. *f*. Ped. *f* (coupled to Gt.).	Prepare: Gt. *ff*. Sw. *mf* plus reeds. Ped. *f* (coupled to Gt.). Sw.-Gt.
Play-over: Melody only (no harmony) first three bars, on strong solo stop on Sw., or if not available, on Gt. solo stop.	*Play-over:* Sw. (no pedals) first three bars. Count 2,3,4 at same speed (lift chord off on 3).
Add: Principal stop to Gt., and Sw.-Gt. coupler, counting 2,3,4 at same speed as play-over (on 3, lift off the B).	
Verse 1: *f* Gt. (coupled to Sw.) plus Ped.	*Verse 1:* *ff* Gt. (coupled to Sw.) plus Ped. For the repeated chords in first and second quarters of tune, hold one part (not Sop.) and repeat others by lifting (detaching) to help the rhythm move.

GOOD CHOIR	CHOIR LACKING CONFIDENCE
Verse 2:	*Verse 2:*
Organ: reduced to *mf* (? Sw. only). *Choir:* Sops.—Descant. Men— Melody.	*Organ* reduced to *f* (still on Gt. with Ped.).
Verse 3:	*Verse 3:*
Choir: unaccompanied. If necessary, play about two chords on Sw., to get the choir started, then fade out. *While the choir is singing:*	either reduced further to *mf*, with Ped., or still *f*, without Ped.
Prepare: Gt. (strong solo stop; e.g. Trpt.) Sw. *f* (including mixtures). Ped. to Sw. (plus heavy 16′).	
Verse 4:	*Verse 4:*
Organ: R.H. melody on Gt. L.H. playing descant plus Alto on Sw. Ped.-Bass. *Choir:* Sops.—Descant. Men— Melody.	*ff* as Verse 1. If descant is possible, then the descant is helped by the arrangement as for "good choir".

Extra touch. Just before the climax of tune (D, last quarter) add stops—e.g. Sw. Reed, or Sw. 8ve., or Sw. 8ve. plus sub 8ve., or Twelfth, or increase weight of pedal (remember to take away also at end of verse).

.   .   .

Sandys (D Major) Five Verses

A Child This Day Is Born or Teach Me My God And King

This tune can be transposed down to C Major, as the high notes are a little high for a congregation which includes men.

GOOD CHOIR	CHOIR LACKING CONFIDENCE
Prepare: Gt. Open Diap. 2, plus light 4′ stop, and 2′ Fifteenth. Sw. 8′, 4′, 2′ stops (no reeds). Ped. *mf*. Sw.—Gt.	**Prepare:** Gt. *f*; 8′, 4′, 2′ (Diapasons). Sw. *mf*; 8′, 4′, 2′. Ped. *f* (coupled to Gt.). Sw.-Gt.

70

Play-over:

with bright phrasing (some *staccato*) first seven notes of tune, as harmonised on Sw. (without Ped.); count 2,3; or 2,3,4 (depending on regular convention in church); lift chord off on 3.

Play-over:

Sw. (no Ped.). In order to end on tonic chord of D major, play (1) whole tune, or (2) first quarter and last quarter of tune, or (3) last half of tune. Bright phrasing with some *staccato* — this is a sprightly tune.

Verse 1:

f Gt. with light Ped. uncoupled. First two chords of tune, R.H. *staccato* for the sake of the rhythm.

Verse 1:

f Gt. (plus Sw.) and *p* (Ped.).

Verse 2:

Gt. reduced (e.g. cut out 2′); reverse Sop. and Alto, playing Alto 8ve. higher above Sop. Otherwise as Verse 1, with light Ped.

Verse 2:

mf; reduce as much as one dares without losing control.

Verse 3:

f Gt., as Verse 1, but without Ped. *At end of verse:* Push in Sw. — Gt.

Verse 3:

Repeat as for Verse 1.

Verse 4:

Choir unaccompanied (if necessary, play about two chords on Sw. to start verse off, then fade out). Organist adds Flute part of his own invention, while Ped. plays light *staccato* bass (similar to *pizzicato* on the double-bass).

Add:
Gt. 8′,4′,2′.

Verse 4:

Repeat as for Verse 2.

Verse 5:

As Verse 1, possibly some more upper work (mixture or Twelfth) — but not too much.

Verse 5:

Repeat as for Verse 1, possibly adding bright mixture or Twelfth. Ped. too might be slightly increased.

N.B. The entry in Verse 1 is not easy after a dominant chord, and this should receive attention at the weekly practice. Alternatively, use the method for "choir lacking confidence".

N.B. If a choir lacks confidence, registration should not change abruptly — it is even sometimes a good idea to reduce *after* a verse has started; the choir tends not to notice once it has got going. Keep the Ped. exactly in time with the hands.

.   .   .

Veni Emmanuel (E Minor) Five Verses

Prepare:
Gt. Open Diap. II, plus Twelfth.
Sw. Oboe.
Ped. 8′ (and 16′ at discretion of organist) coupled to Sw.

Play-over:
If hymn is written in ♩s with bar-lines, mentally turn into ♪s without bar-lines. Play on some solo stop (like oboe) melody only as far as the G (10th note). Give this note two beats, then follow with an E (third below), to give their starting-note. Speed fairly fast, each note say m.m. 100–120. Count 2,3 or 2,3,4, adding 8′ and 4′ to Sw. and oboe off. (E off on "3").

Verse 1:
Gt. *poco f.* (Ped. at discretion of organist).

After verse:
Twelfth off.

Verse 2:
Melody (R.H.) on Gt., L.H. accompanying; chordal scheme on Sw. (Ped. at discretion of organist).
Choir: possibly men only.

After verse:
Add 2′ to Sw.

Verse 3:
R.H. plays chordal scheme (transposed up 8ve. on Sw). L.H. plays melody on Gt. (no Ped.), below accompaniment.
After verse:
Sw. 2′ off.

Verse 4:
Same as Verse 2.
Choir: possibly upper voices only.

Add:
Gt. Twelfth plus mixtures.

Verse 5:
As Verse 1.

Prepare:
Gt. *mf* Diap. (I or II): 4′ and 2′.
Sw. *mf*, 8,′4′.

Play-over:
First two lines of melody on Sw., with accompaniment, no Ped. Speed fairly fast. Count 2,3,4 (chord off on 3, or 2,3).

Verse 1:
Gt. *poco f,* as fast as the congregation can reasonably stand it. Try to keep the gaps between the lines moving.
Gt. to Ped. *Off.*
Sw. to Ped. *Out.*

Verse 2:
Melody on Gt. (R.H.) accompanied by L.H. on Sw.

Verse 3:
Repeat scheme of Verse 1.

Verse 4:
Repeat scheme of Verse 2.

Verse 5:
As Verse 1, but slightly stronger.

At the refrain ("Rejoice, Rejoice") *Add* (e.g. Sw.-Gt., Sw. 8ve., Sw. 8ve. plus sub-8ve., mixtures: or change the scheme of accompaniment. At the end of the verse, remember to take these extra stops off).

.   .   .

In the examples shown, the registration has been principally dictated by the need for variety. Sometimes the words themselves give a hint about the choice of registration. Beware of being over-ingenious; playing softer, for example, every time "death" is mentioned. Go for the sentiment of the whole verse, and give the whole hymn an average type registration, from which one departs, and to which one returns.

METHODS OF PLAYING A FOUR-PART HYMN

The greatest difficulty here for the pianist-turned-organist is to play the bass with the feet. This is, in fact, extremely difficult at first, as the left hand tries to do the same as the feet. There are exercises to help this particular skill in many organ "methods" — e.g. Alcock's *The Organ* (Nov.). If a pianist is "doing his best", that is, playing because he is the only musician available in the vicinity, it may even be advisable to allow the left hand and the feet to take the bass together at first, bearing in mind that a better state of independence will one day be reached. As this is achieved, a hymn should also be practised in the three different ways shown below:

	1	*2*	*3*
RH	SA	S (The tune "stands out").	S (strong stop). Tenor can be omitted as it is often the same as S.
LH	T	AT	Descant plus A.
Pedal	B	B	B (quiet registration).

Artistically this is enough — but further independence can be achieved in other ways. (1) Melody on Ped., ATB with the hands; (2) melody with LH, A and T with RH, B on Ped. This growing independence takes a long time to achieve — several years.

ORGANIST — FOLLOWER OR LEADER?

An assistant organist, on taking his first job in a church, was told

by a regular organist (a lady): "Don't worry about the psalms—
just follow the men. Mr. Hamel is excellent." She was obviously
trying to help, and in one sense her advice was good—*Listen,
Listen, Listen.* But follow—no! If the music in a church is good
rhythmically, it is because the organist makes it so. One must also
remember that most organs speak late in some degree; if the
organist waited for anyone else, there would be a gradual *ritar-
dando* until the music ground to a stop. This must, however, be
qualified slightly. (1) If the choir is excellent, the organist may be
"co-operating" with the choir to keep the rhythm alive (this is
the ideal situation). (2) If the congregation and the organist start
to "come apart", the organist may have to give in slightly until
he has regained control. If an organist knows that he has a bad
sense of pulse, there are a few hints in Chapter Five.

DESCANTS

For the sake of the congregation, it is a good idea if the general
pitch (or *tessitura*) of a hymn does not go up too high (generally
up to D, touching on E flat or E). This means that a soprano's or
treble's top notes are not much used, except in the anthem. One
way out of this problem is to give the top voices a descant; this
also adds variety to a hymn.

A descant can, however, upset a congregation if it is too
powerful or ingenious, unless the melody is equally strongly held.
The organ can help here (see "methods of playing a four-part
hymn"). Sometimes only a few sopranos sing the descant, while
the rest sing the tune.

Properly speaking, there are faux-bourdons and descants. In
faux-bourdons, the hymn-parts are re-arranged so that the tenors
have the melody, while another part is sung by the sopranos. The
altos and basses have their own parts. In a descant, there are two
singing parts—the melody and the descant; the hymn itself
may be (and often is) reharmonised from the original four-part
version.

Most choirmasters who have become proud of their soprano-
line have at some time or another written descants. Many a dull
sermon may have been whiled away with a little elementary two-
part harmony work behind the scenes. Some writers have produced books of descants, or faux-bourdons. These include: Allan

74

Gray (Cambridge, 1929), Cyril Winn (O.U.P.), Maurice Jacobson's *Forty Descants for use with Standard Hymnals* (Cur.), Eric Thiman's *Twenty Faux-Bourdons to Hymns in Common Use* (Bay. & Fer.), and Geoffrey Shaw's *Descant Hymn-Tune Book* (2 vols., Nov.). There are several superb descants in *Songs of Praise*, which most choirs strive to do for some festival occasion. The present writers venture to include two descants which were not composed during sermons.

Immortal, invisible (St. Denio).

Praise my soul (Goss). Descant for last verse harmonisation.

Praise Him, Praise Him, Praise the ev-er - la - - - sting King.

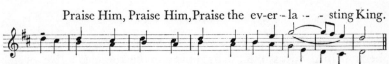

A descant should not be merely "correct two-part harmony", but should have a shape of its own, with properly constructed climaxes, and should to some extent be complementary to the original tune, bearing in mind at the same time that a congregation can be upset by too much diversity. The occasional "long note" ("catching up" the words afterwards) greatly enhances a descant.

NEW HYMN TUNES

These must be introduced from time to time. If the choir is good and properly rehearsed, this can be done without much difficulty. It is suggested (1) that the support of the minister is first obtained, and that the new tune is announced with a *positive* approach. "This hymn tune will not be familiar to most of you, but as we are a forward-looking church, etc., etc."; (2) that the organist plays the tune complete at the play-over on some very obvious solo stop, the other parts ATB accompanying; (3) that the first (or first two) verses are sung in unison, and also the last. Perhaps one or two verses in harmony would be enough at the first appearance. In the ensuing weeks, this new tune should be systematically repeated, once every two or three weeks, until it begins to be familiar.

There will always be members of the congregation who object to a new tune: "I'm not a stick-in-the-mud myself, but it seems such a pity when there is a perfectly good tune that has stood the test of the years"; "I quite like it myself, but it's much too difficult for the congregation to get hold of." If the organist can have a good-natured reply ready: "I quite agree with you myself, but I think the younger members . . .", or if he finds it difficult to be good-natured, he can always ask the critic to refer the complaint to the minister. It is only fair to remember that not every new hymn tune is necessarily better than an older one. On the other hand many tunes become out-of-date as tastes change, and not every *old* tune is a good one.

CONGREGATIONAL PRACTICE

A new tune is accepted more willingly if the congregation has been helped to assimilate it. This can be done (1) five or ten minutes before the service; (2) at some suitable point in the service (with the minister's permission); (3) after the service. The last is not very satisfactory as people tend to go home to "cook the joint" and "get calves out of pits", etc. If the organist has the choir with him in the pews, congregational practice can be quite simple and effective — the congregation should be treated good-naturedly — not as an inferior type of church choir.

A congregational practice may also help to "boost" the singing of the congregation. If, despite the attempts of the choir and its choirmaster (possibly owing to the acoustics of the building) the congregation will not sing with confidence and enthusiasm, some members of the choir can be scattered at various strategic points in the congregation for a few weeks. If this has a good effect, the members should not be withdrawn too suddenly. A congregation is of course helped much more effectively by a choir singing behind them: i.e. with a choir in the gallery (with, ideally, the organist as well, on a detached console). A congregation may also be helped to realise its responsibility if it sings verses alternately with the choir.

METRICAL HYMN-PSALMS

As an alternative to psalm-chanting, one can use a metrical hymn-psalm. Some of these "versifications" of the psalms are good; many of them stretch back to the sixteenth century. There are at least three well-known versions of Psalm 23; perhaps not everyone realises, for example, that "All people that on earth do dwell" is a "versification" of Psalm 100. Let us be honest, however, and admit that some of these psalms are weak—perhaps "doggerel" is a little too forceful, but they tend this way. Trouble often arises over forced rhyming. As long as the words fit a well-known tune metrically, is it necessary for them to rhyme? Good poets, please, there is still some useful work for you here; some metrical verse of higher quality is needed.

THE ANTHEM

This can be another example of verse set to music. If the text of the anthem can be made to fit the theme of the Sunday, so much the better. This is where liaison between the organist and the minister is so essential—and so often lacking. The *Churchman's Kalendar* (Mowbray) gives details of (Church of England) Lessons, etc., throughout the year, and this may be useful. Rehearsal of the anthem is discussed in Chapter Six.

CHAPTER FOUR

THE ORGAN (INSTRUMENT)

The organ is an expensive and inspiring instrument. There are many who feel it is too expensive. Against this, however, one must remember that the length of life of an organ is probably the longest of any mechanical instrument. There are some instruments on the Continent which date from 1600 or 1700, with only a few minor restorations during the period of time. Some organs in England have been in use for well over one hundred years. And there are few better instruments, playable by one man, for leading the singing of a large number of people in the worship of God. There are other people who feel that the organ is too inspiring — that there is a danger of confusing the worship of God with the worship of the instrument; it would be a sad thing, however, to lose some of the world's great music, which was expressly written for the organ, music which can help to condition the minds and spirits of worshippers — to reflect inwardly, rejoice outwardly or, by following the growth of some larger work, to become more aware of the architectural achievements of which an inspired composer is capable.

GENERAL PRINCIPLES OF CONSTRUCTION

The basic principles of construction are fairly simple. The organist plays on the *Console*, which has one or more manuals (usually the limit is five). A *Manual* is a row of 61-odd black and white keys, and is similar to a piano keyboard, though approximately two octaves shorter. The manuals (or "organs" as they are sometimes called) have different names — *Great, Swell, Choir*, and the larger organs may also have *Echo* and *Solo* manuals.* Once in a while one comes across manuals which are coloured the wrong way round — black notes for white, and white for black — but this has no great significance.

* The manuals on a three-manual British organ are arranged with the Swell at the top, the Great in the middle, and the Choir at the bottom. On a five-manual organ the order (from top to bottom) would be: Echo, Solo, Swell, Great, Choir.

French, German and Italian equivalents for the manuals are:

English	French	German	Italian
Great Organ	Grand'orgue	Hauptwerk	Grand'organo
Swell Organ	Récit	Oberwerk	Organo d'espressione
Choir Organ	Positif	Positiv	Organo di coro

There is a further set of keys (about two-and-a-half octaves only) which are played by the feet—this is called the *Pedal-board* (or *Pedal Organ*). In older organs the pedal-board was straight and the keys parallel; later the board was made concave with the keys radiating, and thus easier for the feet to play upon.

Surrounding the manuals—usually to the left and right, but sometimes above as well—are the *Drawstops*; these are pulled out (drawn) and pushed in (usual abbreviation "off"). The name of the stop and its pitch is usually engraved on the stop knob which is fitted to the end of the rod. Most of the older organs have drawstops; the cinema organ introduced *Tabs* or *Stop-Keys* which are flicked up or down instead of being pulled out or pushed in. These became a fashion for the church organ also. Each stop (or tab) connects with a complete set of pipes of a particular timbre. Until a stop is pulled out, no note will sound. Various stops are connected with particular manuals: on an English organ, for example, the Great might have a group of *Diapason* stops comprising: Double Open Diapason 16', Open Diapason I 8', Open Diapason II 8', Principal 4', Twelfth 2¾', Fifteen 2', Mixtures three ranks. Diapason is the "basic" tone of an English church organ—the tone which most listeners would accept as characteristic of the instrument. A smaller organ may have a selection of these diapason stops, and a larger organ still more diapasons. All these stops have basically the same type of sound. The 16', 8', 4', etc., refers to the length of the pipes controlled by a particular stop, and therefore the pitch. A 16' stop will sound an octave below the actual pitch of the written note; an 8' stop at actual pitch; a 4' stop an octave higher; a 2' stop two octaves higher. The "Twelfth" is a *Mutation Stop*, sounding an octave-plus-a-fifth higher than the actual note.

Mixtures (or *Mixture Stops*) have several ranks of pipes, the pitches of which correspond to certain of the upper partials* (or

* These upper partials, together with the lowest, or fundamental, note, are known collectively as the Harmonic Series. A tube with a fundamental note two octaves

79

harmonics) of the note which is being played. The methods of
tuning these notes may vary on different organs; as an example, a
mixture (3 ranks) might give sounds a twelfth, fifteenth and
nineteenth above the note played. In combination with other
stops, Mutation and Mixture stops add brightness and brilliance.

TONE-COLOUR OF STOPS

There are other types of sound produced by different stops. For
example, *Flute* stops are usually made of wood or metal, and work
on the same principle as the Diapason: i.e. a penny whistle.
There are names such as Hohlflöte, Rohrflöte, Spitzflöte, Claribel
Flute, Waldflöte, Harmonic Flute, Piccolo, Flageolet.

Reed stops have considerably more edge and penetrating power.
The pipes for these stops are made with a vibrating metal tongue
which sets a column of air in motion. The commonest names are
Oboe, Bassoon (Fagotto), Trumpet (Tromba), Clarion, Clarinet,
Cor Anglais, Cornopean, Tuba, Posaune, Horn. A few other stops
do not belong to any of the three main families: e.g. Dulciana,
Voix Celeste, Vox Angelica, Viole d'orchestre, Viola da Gamba;
these are of another quality, sometimes labelled "string tone".

As we have said, each manual has an associated number of
stops. The Great is usually considered the most powerful, has
most of the diapason stops, may have a Dulciana, some flute
stops, and possibly a reed or two (e.g. a trumpet or tuba). The
Swell generally has a few diapason stops of a quieter variety, some
flute stops, and a good selection of reeds. Occasionally the combined reeds of the Swell may almost equal the Great in volume.
The Choir often contains an attractive selection of flute stops (e.g.
8', 4' and 2'), and has some reed stops which can be used as
quieter solo stops (e.g. Clarinet, Cor Anglais); it may also have
some stops of a colourless type for accompanying. The Pedal at

---

below middle C vibrates not only as a whole, but also in halves, thirds, quarters, etc.,
to produce a Harmonic Series as follows:

Fundamental Note

1 2 3 4 5 6 7 8 9 10 11 12 13 14 15 16

Nos. 7, 11, 13, 14 (enclosed in brackets) are slightly out of tune.

its worst may have two 16′ stops—Bourdon 16′ and Open Diapason 16′—one muffled and indistinct, the other often heavy, though clearer. At its best the Pedal may have a complete chorus of diapasons, flutes and reeds at 16′, 8′ and 4′ pitch, and even mixtures as well.

The pipes connected to the Swell manual are usually enclosed in a box. One side of this box has shutters which can be opened or closed, increasing or decreasing the volume. A mechanism usually connects these shutters with the player's right foot; this is called the *Swell Pedal*. When an organist stops playing, these shutters should be left open, so that air can pass freely through so as to equalise the temperatures—otherwise the Swell stops tend to get out of tune with the rest of the organ.

The Choir pipes may also be enclosed, and have shutters workable by the left foot (*Choir Pedal*).

If there is a third pedal, this may be the *Crescendo Pedal* referred to in the section which follows.

Although each manual has an associated set of stops, these can be made playable on another manual with the aid of *Couplers* (these resemble stops, but are actually devices for combining different sounds). By drawing "Swell to Great", the Swell stops are made available on the Great. By drawing "Great to Pedal", the Great stops sound when played by the feet on the pedalboard. Another form of coupler is the "Octave" and "Suboctave"—these produce the note at normal pitch, together with the note an octave higher or lower. Both can be used together, producing three notes for each one played. To this can be added a device called "Unison off". This removes the 8′ tone (i.e. the sound of the note at normal pitch), leaving the octave above and below without its "parent" note in the middle. This "unison off" needs to be used with care; if drawn by accident, many notes mysteriously refuse to sound. Another device which may be potentially dangerous is the Crescendo Pedal. This adds stops automatically in a certain planned order, and there is a similar device for subtracting stops. These devices (which are not found on the normal small organ) can give an unwary organist a shock or two if he does not realise that they are in action.

In order to pull out stops, or flick down tabs, one of the organist's hands must momentarily desert the keys. If, however, this is impossible, he may use the *Pistons* which are to be found on most organs. These pistons, which are numbered 1, 2, 3, 4, etc., usually relate to quantity of tone ($1 = p$, $2 = mp$, $3 = mf$, etc.), but they can be associated with timbre or even some particular solo stop. Not all organists realise that the organ-builder or tuner can change these pistons to suit individual taste. There may also be a set of pistons for the feet. By pulling out the "Great Pistons to Pedal", one gets a balanced choice of pedal stops coming out as the Great Pistons are adjusted. The hand pistons are usually arranged under the particular manual with which they are associated; in this way they can be worked by the thumb, while the fingers continue to play.

More modern organs occasionally have *Pre-Selection Pistons*. Before beginning a recital, the organist plans a choice of stops he needs at various critical moments, and sets his pistons to produce exactly those stops.

There is also the famous "Tremulant" stop, which produces an uneven flow of wind. Used with care and artistry (especially on soft stops) this is a most useful stop addition. A slightly similar effect is obtained by using the Voix Celeste with another soft stop. The Voix Celeste is usually tuned slightly sharper or flatter than the other stops; the result is a waving effect which may be pleasant if used with discrimination.

THE WIND-SYSTEM

The way in which the key, when depressed, makes a pipe sound is basically very simple, though when entered into in greater detail it becomes more complicated. The *Blower* creates a continual wind pressure which is carried to all parts of the organ. (The amount of wind pressure is an important factor.) When a stop is drawn, the air is "diverted" to a particular set of pipes, and when a particular key is depressed, a hole is opened which allows air to enter that particular pipe. There are many reasons why air finds it difficult to enter a pipe. (1) The blower may not be working.

(2) The slide which emits air to the whole rank of pipes may be stiff, and refuse to move. (3) The pipe may not be sitting exactly in position (if replaced carelessly by some amateur). (4) The pipe may be blocked by dirt. (5) The action connecting the key to the pipe may be broken or disconnected. An organ-builder could probably list another thirty reasons; most of the above problems are really his province, but an intelligent organist with a practical frame of mind can sometimes do something useful.

ACTIONS

There are several *Actions*. Action is the name for the way in which the key is connected with the pallets which admit the wind to the pipe.

The original method is called *Tracker* action, which connects the player directly, "physically", with the sound. Many organists prefer this feeling of direct contact, though when couplers are used the sheer physical power used to press down several levers at once can become very tiring, and as the mechanism becomes worn, the clatter may become greater than the music. There is a returning preference for Tracker action, as modern levers have reduced the physical effort, which was its chief defect.

Pneumatic action considerably lightens the load, though the notes may tend to "speak" late. This means that an organist with this type of action has to play in front of the beat—following a conductor means anticipating a conductor, and becomes almost an intuitive act.

With *Electro-Pneumatic* action the response is quicker. One now has enormous quantities of wires, and the success of the action depends largely on electrical "contacts".

When the *Console* (i.e. the unit containing the keyboards, pedal-board, stops, etc.) is *detached* from the rest of the organ (to which it is connected by wires), the organist may find it easier to hear the result of his playing, but he will have to bear in mind the time-lag between the pressing-down of a key and the sound reaching his ears. This may be quite appreciable if the console is some distance from the pipes.

The organ-builder is generally responsible for tuning and maintenance; but there are occasions when an organist could attend to some defect on his own account. Perhaps the worst trouble, needing immediate attention, is a *Cipher*. This can occur during a hymn — one particular note or pipe will not stop sounding. The immediate solution is to switch off the blower, and at the first available opportunity one can try to deal with the fault. Is the key sticking? The cipher would then occur on all stops on that particular manual. Temporarily one can push in all stops on that manual, and avoid using it. The fault might be stiffness (e.g. dampness making wood or felts swell), or it might be electrical — some contact may not be separating, or some wire may be touching another. The fault might be at the "pipe-end"; if so, the best way is to locate the pipe (aurally, or by putting one's hand over the pipes to feel for escaping air), and then to lift the particular pipe gently out of its socket, and stuff some rag in the hole to avoid the sound of escaping air. This must be done with care.

One or two individual notes on a particular stop may get so badly out of tune that an organist scarcely dares to use that stop. If so, and it is impossible to obtain a professional tuner, he could try to tune the offending notes. For this he really needs an assistant; but if no one is available there are ways of putting weights (? hymn books) on individual notes, which then continue to sound while the organist goes into the organ-loft. Each stop is tuned to one basic stop — usually the *Principal* on the Great, so one really needs two weights, one on E (for example) on the Principal, and the other on the offending E. (If the offending E is an 8′ stop, the Principal E will have to be an octave lower, as the Principal is a 4′ stop.) It will then be discovered that there is a considerable wave (or vibrato) between the notes. As one tunes the offending note, the wave gradually slows down, and should be finally eliminated. The basic stop (the Principal) is itself tuned in octaves to its own central octave. This should not be interfered with by an amateur; it is tuned in equal temperament, and this is a skilled job.

The method of tuning varies from one family of pipes to another. Wooden flutes have a metal flap on top, which can be raised or lowered. "Stopped" pipes, which are blocked at the top, can be tuned by raising or lowering their stoppers—the block may have a small handle attached to the top. Reed-pipes can be tuned by raising or lowering the tuning-wire which sits in a "block" near the base of the pipe. This allows more or less of the "tongue" to vibrate. Metal Flue-pipes (e.g. Diapason) are tuned by brass cones—like small dunce's caps. To sharpen the pitch one opens up the top by tapping the pointed end of the cone into the pipe; by using the cone the other way up, the pipe is closed up. Unless one has these cones, one should resist the temptation to bend the top of the pipe (or open it up) by hand; the top of the pipe will quickly deteriorate if this is done. Some pipes are tuned with "slides" which open or close slots in the pipe, thus shortening or lengthening the air column. This method is really better than the cone one.

The pipes in an organ-loft are not usually arranged chromatically; one common method is to find them left and right in two whole-tone families—C, D, E, F sharp, G sharp, B flat on one side, the rest on the other. This has the effect of equalising weights, and attractive symmetrical pipe-patterns can be made.

Escaping air is another trouble from which all organs are liable to suffer. This can be due to excessive dryness of atmosphere, and organ-builders recommend that pails of water should be placed near the blower, and in the organ-loft, to increase humidity. In dry atmospheres leather can become less pliable, and crack; this may lead to further troubles. Actual leaks which can be clearly located (for example, in the large pipe carrying air to the organ pipes) can, of course, be cured with patches and "impact" glue. The organ should be switched off until the glue is thoroughly dry.

Small old organs with very noisy actions can be re-washered with felt washers; this is really a job for the professional organ-builder. The result is well worth the trouble taken.

ELECTRONIC ORGANS

In the electronic organ the sounds, instead of coming from vibrating reeds, are built up directly from oscillating electric currents. Thus it is possible to produce synthetic sound-waves not only of measurable pitch, but also with a timbre (or quality) closely resembling that of different orchestral instruments.

Several types of electronic organs have been made (Hammond,

Compton, Lowrey, Miller, etc.); in some the tone is generated from tone-wheels, in others from valves. Sometimes transistors are used for generators in place of valves; this enables the organ to remain in tune if there is a voltage drop in the mains supply.

Electronic organs range from one-manual models, with self-contained amplifier and speakers, to "cathedral" models with two manuals, pedal-boards, and separate reverberation systems designed to reproduce the acoustics of a large concert hall. The price range (1967) is in the region of £300 to £3,000. Examples: a small two-manual organ with a conventional console (specification 61-note Great with seven stops, 61-note Swell with seven stops, and 32-note pedal-board with four stops) can be bought for about £650. A fairly large two-manual organ (six couplers, two independent ranks of generators, and three sound channels) will cost £1,500 or so.

Is the electronic organ suitable for the church? The leaflet *Electronic Organs* (The Church Information Office) expresses the view that not only is the electronic organ musically inferior to the pipe organ but also, compared to a pipe organ, it is not really cheap. Although the initial cost of a pipe organ may be greater, it says, its probable life would appear to be about twice as long as that of an electronic organ; and at the end of its life the electronic organ will need to be replaced, whereas the pipe organ can be rebuilt at a cost lower than that of a new instrument. Similar views are expressed in the leaflet *The Church Organ* (published by the (Roman Catholic) Church Music Association); this useful leaflet also deals with the design, specification and installation of pipe organs.

Nevertheless, a good many electronic organs have been installed in churches, chapels and schools, and there are certainly more to come. Before the decision to instal an electronic organ is taken, however, expert advice should be sought to ensure that the sound is as pipe-like and decisive as possible.

An unlooked-for hazard was reported in *The Times* of 2 July 1965; an electronic organ in a Hampshire church has added radio messages from passing police cars or ambulances to the hymns that are being played.

Expert advice on the installation of an organ in a new church, or the rebuilding or replacement of an existing organ, can be obtained from the Secretary, Organs Advisory Committee, 5

Great College Street, London, S.W.1, or alternatively from cathedral organists, organ consultants and organ-building firms of high repute.

As with clothes, so with organs there are fashions—in registration. Registration means combining the different sounds available to the organist in certain ways. In the Victorian era, sheer weight of sound was very much admired—"the mighty organ"; today there is a growing appreciation of neo-baroque sound, and a desire to return to the sounds made by earlier organs; the ideal now perhaps is clarity of sound, with a preference for upper work (twelfths, mixtures, etc.) as opposed to weighty 8' and 16', the boomy bass being quite out of fashion. A tailor who insisted on cutting his clothes in the style of ten years ago would soon be out of business—similarly an organist must move with the times.

But behind the demands of fashion, there are certain reasonably basic principles, in the same way as cloth has certain basic properties. (Even here, though, the advent of Terylene, nylon, etc., can change some of these properties.)

From the sound, as opposed to the constructional point of view, there may be said to be three families of stops: Diapasons, Flutes, Reeds. There is a further family called Strings, though whether any pipe worked by air will ever produce a sound like that of a stringed instrument is open to question; but this is meant to describe certain pipe stops (e.g. Viola da Gamba) which are flue-pipes and yet have a different sound to diapasons and flutes.

Each family can have stops of 16', 8', 4', 2' quality, and mutation stops in addition (see page 79). On a small organ, there will of course be only a selection of these.

REGISTRATION ON ONE MANUAL

The first basic type of registration may be called: using the stops of *one family only*.

The most ordinary tone possible would be produced on an 8' stop alone. To this could be added a 4' stop (of the same family). This would add brightness. A 2' stop could then be added to give more brightness. One could now add a 16' stop; this would add thickness and weight, while slightly reducing the clarity. Now one might add a twelfth, mixtures, etc., increasing the brilliance, but slightly reducing the exactness of pitch. (It becomes less easy to say: "That chord is DBG", as other harmonic notes are mixed up with these three notes.) When a Bach fugue, for example, has editorial suggestions ("Reduce", "Add", etc.) one could add or subtract stops on the above method.

There are other possibilities, of course. (1) Leave out one of the stops. Try 8' + 2' tone, 16' + 4' tone, etc. (2) Leave out two stops. Try 16' + 2', 8' + mixtures.

The second type of registration is obtained by *mixing the families*. Here taste plays an enormous part. Some organists do not approve of mixing flutes and diapasons. But on some organs, for example, Open Diapason II (8') goes excellently with Harmonic Flute (4'). If a particular sound pleases your ear, it is a good sound (for you). If everybody objects to it, however, it would perhaps be wiser to ask a friend to play a few notes with that particular combination, and listen to it in the church, away from the instrument; the effect may not then appear so good. Even a very small organ has many possibilities, within the range of its one manual. If an organist finds that he is using only stereotyped combinations, let him invite an enterprising friend to come and play on his instrument, carefully saying nothing about his own registration beforehand.

Diapasons produce a firm solid sound, flutes have charm, reeds have penetration and power. The Tremulant (used extensively on cinema and electronic organs) produces another "family" of sounds. These are not necessarily in bad taste, and can be used at varying pitches and in various dynamics.

COMBINING TWO MANUALS

Suppose the organ is a two-manual one—Swell and Great. By using the Swell-Great Coupler the stops on the Swell can be used on the Great. This means, for example, that the Mixture stop on the Swell (if it is a good stop) can be combined with various Great stops with better effect than if the Mixture on the Great (possibly a powerful stop) were used. So, when one wishes to add the Swell Mixture to a combination on the Great, one either pulls out the Swell-Great Coupler (the Mixture being prepared), or one pulls out the Swell Mixture (the Swell-Great Coupler being out).

When combining various sounds, one becomes aware of the

88

difference between one organ and another. Organs which are tonally good have greater capacity for good blend. It would not be possible, of course, for all stops to blend, but perfection is probably nearest when all stops are drawn, and only one sound can be heard, rather than, say, many different sounds standing apart from one another.

OPPOSING TWO MANUALS

(1) *In volume.* This arrangement is most useful for the playover and first verse of a hymn, but is also the standard arrangement for any work in the baroque period, which presumed a loud and a less loud manual.

If one wishes to have the same family of stops on both manuals, the Swell stops are generally softer than those on the Great — so *Swell*, diapasons 8' and 4': *Great*, diapasons 8' and 4', and one has a balance *mf-f*. By closing the Swell Box this difference might be increased to *mp-f*.

(2) *In stop-quality, but volume similar.* For example: *Swell*, diapasons: *Great*, flutes. Carefully balance. A good way to do this is to play, for example, middle C on Swell, middle E on Great. Then reverse. It may be necessary to change the stops slightly, but it may be equally possible to balance with the Swell Pedal. This arrangement is useful for Trio Sonatas (the Pedal producing the third voice).

(3) *In stop-quality and volume.* Here there is no balancing to be done; the main aim is to achieve contrast. Even more contrast is obtained if one manual uses (for example) 8' + 4' + 2', while the other uses only 8' stops. The degree of contrast required is again a question of taste, and needs much thought.

(4) *For a solo with accompaniment.* The solo will probably be single notes; the accompaniment may consist of chords of two, three, or even four notes. Therefore one must take considerable care that the accompaniment is always softer than the solo. This is where certain colourless stops (e.g. Dulciana) are so useful. (The accompaniment can also be too soft — this is equally unsatisfactory.)

With three manuals there is a very simple trick for making two solo stops with accompaniment available (without change of stops). A solo stop on the Swell (not a reed) may be accompanied by a colourless stop on the Choir. Another solo stop on the Great can then be accompanied by the Swell. This means a little juggling with the hands.

MORE THAN TWO MANUALS

The same principles as above apply, but the possibilities—in combination and contrast—are enormously increased.

THE PEDAL

The Pedal can be:

(1) *An independent part*. As, for example, in a Trio Sonata—see (2) on p. 89. The Pedal needs careful balancing against the other two parts; it should not of course be coupled to either of the manuals if possible; it should not have 16′ tone if possible; if the organ has three manuals it can of course be coupled to the unused manual, if this will give clearer pitch definition. Pedal stops are often woolly or boomy. It may even be better to use no Pedal stops at all, and to couple to this third manual.

(2) *The foundation to the sound-structure*. It should then be coupled to the basic-registration, and have fundamentally the same type sound; the degree of 4′, 8′, 16′, 32′ tone depending on taste.

(3) *The solo part*. It will need careful balancing (especially if the rest of the organ is *f*) to make sure that it "gets through" with clear pitch definition. It may need some cunning coupling to a manual—even using 4′ and 2′, or a Mixture stop.

(4) *The foundation of the accompaniment* (4) page 89. The Pedal should generally be coupled to the accompanying manual, and a soft 16′ (+8′) Pedal stop used.

SWELL OCTAVE, SUB-OCTAVE, AND UNISON OFF

SWELL OCTAVE (SW. 8VE)

Reproduces the same sounds an octave higher. Therefore in a sense doubles the number of stops. Although it is often used to increase the brightness of some fairly loud combination, experiments should be made of combining with single stops: e.g. Stopped Diapason + Swell 8ve: 8′ Trumpet + Swell 8ve, etc.

SWELL SUB-OCTAVE (SW. SUB.)

Reproduces the same sounds an octave lower. The same remarks apply as above. Try Fifteenth + Swell Sub-Octave: 8' Trumpet + Swell Sub-Octave.

SWELL OCTAVE + SUB-OCTAVE

Adds weight and brightness, at least doubling the tone, and is therefore very effective. Try this on all the reeds by themselves.

SWELL UNISON OFF + SWELL OCTAVE + SUB-OCTAVE

Removes all 8' tone, but leaves behind the 16' and 4' tone of each stop. Be very wary of pulling out the "Unison Off" by mistake!

PRACTISING AND PAYING FOR ELECTRICITY

For the sake of harmony with the Hon. Treasurer of the Parish, the organist should discuss what fee per hour should be paid for practice. The organist himself, of course, practises without payment, but his pupils will also want to practise. One way is for the pupils to time themselves, and to write down in a book how long they have practised. This implies honesty on the part of a pupil, but it is very difficult to think of a better way—and most organ students are responsible people. If the organ is locked, each pupil will need a key. An organ student who becomes thoroughly useful may in fact become assistant organist, playing for occasional services, accompanying anthems, and playing while the regular organist is on holiday, etc. In these circumstances he might be allowed to practise free. Pupils should be actively discouraged from practising *forte*—this is very irritating to solitary worshippers, church cleaners, etc.

THE CARE AND MAINTENANCE OF THE ORGAN

An organ, like a piano, needs to be properly cared for, and to be played upon often enough to keep it in good condition. Regular servicing and tuning is necessary, and it is best to make a contract with an organ-builder (if possible the builder of the organ) to carry out this work at least two, and preferably three or four, times a year. In addition, the action should have a major overhaul every fifteen years or so. It is a good plan for the organist, between tunings, to keep written notes of any mechanical faults

91

which may appear so that they can be brought to the notice of the tuner.

The method of heating and ventilating a church needs careful consideration: excessive damp on the one hand, and excessive dryness on the other, may cause damage to the organ. Particular care should be taken if a gas heating system is installed; a useful leaflet on this subject, *Gas Heating in Churches*, may be obtained from The Central Council for the Care of Churches, Fulham Place, London, S.W.6. Other, and often more satisfactory, methods of heating are described in *Church Heating Today* (The Church Information Office).

CHAPTER FIVE

THE ORGANIST (HUMAN BEING)

This chapter opens with a short section on the problems of learning to play the organ. As most people approach the organ from the piano, one should be aware of the essential differences between piano technique and organ technique. It is true that there are ten fingers to discipline on a keyboard (or manual) in playing both instruments. It is also true that all the subtleties of *staccato* and *legato* apply equally—possibly a little more noticeably on the organ—but after this, the main similarities cease. It might be useful to list the main differences.

VOLUME

There is a direct connection on the piano between touch (speed of key-depression) and volume. To play "expressively" means, largely, to vary touch. On the organ, volume is controlled primarily by registration (manipulation of stops), secondarily by the use of the Swell-pedal (also Choir-pedal and Crescendo-pedal if these exist). Variation of speed of key-depression has no effect (except, of course, that some organs have light actions, and some very heavy ones).

LEGATO

A pianist can always help his *legato* with the sustaining-pedal. Pedalling can simplify awkward fingering. On the organ, an unwanted break between notes cannot be "saved" by anything; if *legato* is required, this may necessitate complicated fingering—especially the changing of fingers on a held note. A pianist who changes to organ nearly always sounds like a beginner because his *legato* is so poor. Simple hymns in particular sound rough and jerky.

TECHNIQUE

A pianist feels that he is progressing as he learns to play faster, and as his control of dynamics widens. The organist's problem is primarily one of co-ordination: (1) to co-ordinate feet and hands (especially "separating" LH and feet); (2) to co-ordinate control of the stops as well. There are in fact four—not three—co-ordinations.

FOLLOWING A CONDUCTOR

This is much easier on the piano than on the organ. An organist usually has to use mirrors—and is happier with a friend to relay the beat.

HEARING THE RESULT

Some organists who are badly placed hardly ever hear their organ as it really sounds. It may, in addition, speak late. The ideal of the detached console is an expensive business—nevertheless it is worth aiming for!

Despite these differences, most organists prefer to have a pupil who has already acquired some skill on the piano. In this way, one (at least) of the necessary co-ordinations is partly established.

At what age should this change-over take place? Preferably not too late. Some children find co-ordination a relatively simple affair; very few adults find it easy to add "extra dimensions" to the brain. Try to reach a level of about Grade V (Associated Board) on the piano, and then begin; at any age from, say, ten onwards.

Then, don't hurry. Establish the new co-ordinations gradually and slowly. The problems are:

TO LEARN TO PLAY LEGATO

Practise exercises like the changing-finger exercise in Chapter Three (page 68). This is a problem for the hands only, at first. It entails good listening. But it can be combined with some stop-manipulation. Insist that every repetition of an exercise is done with a different stop (or combination of stops), and that this change is effected *in time* (e.g. counting eight beats, or six, or four, or less).

VARIETY OF STACCATO AND LEGATO

This may need much attention or none—depending on the quality of the previous piano-teacher. This is for the hands only at first.

FEET BY THEMSELVES

Learn to find the notes by "feel". (Hands should have done this already, especially when learning to sight-read.) One feels, of course, for the gaps between the black-note keys, and uses them as a guide. Some teachers allow their pupils to watch their feet.

COMBINING RIGHT HAND AND PEDAL

Ideally, little exercises written for this combination should be practised—but hymns, etc. (SAB) are always suitable.

LEFT HAND AND PEDAL

As above. This is one of the hardest things. Most organ methods have specially written exercises for this.

HANDS ON DIFFERENT MANUALS

Very simple two-part pieces. The piece begins, say, RH on Great, LH on Swell (stops carefully balanced, equal in volume, though different in sound). At specified points the hands come together on one manual (say both to Great), then separate the other way round (LH on Great, RH on Swell), then both together on Swell, then both jump to Great, etc.

If, in all the above exercises, a special point has been made of varying the stops for each repetition, one of the four co-ordinations is being tackled all the time, and needs no special exercises.

These exercises need to be short, and constantly advancing. But few pupils will be content with exercises only; they must have pieces as well—and rightly so! The following books are most helpful:

The Organ, Alcock (Nov. Primer No. 80), contains excellent advice and large numbers of exercises and graded pieces.

The First Year at the Organ, Percy Buck (S. & B.), is similar to the above, but slightly shorter.

Metodo per Organo, F. Germani (4 vols., de Santis, Roma). A huge comprehensive work for the serious organist.

95

Also of interest is: Bach, *Technique of Organ Pedalling* (as shown in his works), edited by H. Coates (Ashdown).

The pieces in the list of voluntaries on pages 98–101 marked with an **E** are relatively easy, and could serve as pieces for beginners.

Some beginner-organists may find colossal difficulties in learning a piece.

(1) The piece is probably too difficult; change it.

(2) Is the organist tackling any technical problems (exercises on pages 94–95) which might help him?

(3) If the piece *must* be learnt despite the tremendous difficulty, a routine of practice needs to be set up. This is a suggestion:

(*a*) Learn so much a day (e.g. if the piece is four pages long, perhaps half a page a day).

(*b*) Split the daily quantity into sections (say, 2–3 bars to a section). Finger it first, and work through from section to section, until the daily dose has been mastered.

(*c*) If it will not go right, call out the co-ordination aloud to help concentration. There are twelve possibilities: (i) *Right* (= right hand alone); (ii) *Left*; (iii) *Right Foot*; (iv) *Left Foot*; (v) *Hands* (right hand + left hand, no pedals); (vi) *Right* and *Right Foot*; (vii) *Left* and *Left Foot*; (viii) *Right* and *Left Foot*; (ix) *Left* and *Right Foot*; (x) *Hands* and *Right Foot*; (xi) *Hands* and *Left Foot*; (xii) *Hands* and *Both Feet*. For each note, one calls out one of the above. If preferred, one can simplify by leaving out Right or Left Foot, thus reducing the number of co-ordinations to seven (*Right*; *Left*; *Foot*; *Hands*; *Right* and *Foot*; *Left* and *Foot*; *All Together*). This is perhaps wiser if a little less thorough. The main thing is to keep the mind moving and prevent that "clogged" feeling, when one forgets what one is trying to do.

(*d*) Having spent eight (or whatever it is) days working through every note of the piece (a slow process), one then goes through again with the aim of *fluency*. Many passages will seem to be as bad as ever, in which case one resolutely repeats the co-ordination discipline, but in time the human brain (a truly amazing machine) begins to smooth over some of the difficulties—*provided* that the basic work has been well done (methodically, good fingering, good co-ordination, practising done in rhythm).

(*e*) If one finds one is bad at the discipline ("I start all right, but after three days I seem to lose interest—there's nothing wrong with the piece—it's just that I've got so much on") the only solution is to find a teacher who will help. Preferably a tyrant.

VOLUNTARIES

An organist may need a voluntary before a service, and one after. He may play quietly during communion. If there are two services, he may need four or five voluntaries each Sunday—if there are three services, he may need six or seven. No wonder a congregation may hear some occasional repetitions!

But repetitions are not necessarily bad. They may need judicious spacing out; but many a fine piece of music needs several hearings. This is, however, why it is so important that the music should be good stuff, and why it should be well played if it is to be repeated many times. Organists, do not lower your standards— play the best music you know, and if you think something is rubbish, don't play it. You may of course be wrong, especially with modern music; one should not be afraid to experiment.

A word about the choice of voluntaries. Before a service, people are gathering, some are praying, some are waiting (some may be talking); the music does not want to be arresting or exciting—it is preparatory, reflective, beautiful. During the communion it should suit the solemnness of the moment, very quiet or beautiful. After the service is the moment for the great fugue, the paean of praise, or the arresting piece of modern music. Another very important consideration is the congregation. Perhaps two people are getting married who are musical enthusiasts—don't trot out Handel's Largo again; perhaps that piece by Reger which one never dares to bring out will be what they want (perhaps not!). If the congregation consists entirely of sleepy old-age pensioners, put the Reger away; out comes Handel's Largo and is enormously appreciated. Perhaps it is your regular congregation, Sunday by Sunday; you cannot give them Handel's *Berenice*, it would be the third time this month; perhaps one of the Eight Easy Preludes (J. S. Bach)? Looking ahead, you know the church will be full for the Bishop's Confirmation in six weeks' time—could you do the Toccata from the Toccata and Fugue in D Minor (J. S. Bach)? —see notes on page 96 on how to learn a piece, despite difficulties.

It would be quite impossible to make an adequate list of

voluntaries; the field is enormous. But in view of the fact that many organists play such poor, uninteresting music before and after services we append here a list of voluntaries, which includes many transcriptions. A little note to ministers: if you wish to encourage your organist to widen his field, get the Hon. Treasurer to give you a small grant of money, and buy some music for your organist. The sight of the bright clean music (not too much at a time) will certainly act as an incentive for learning it. Organists are not paid very much as a rule, and this may make them appear a little stingy about buying new music.

Some Suggestions for Voluntaries

(**E** = Easy)

BAROQUE

BACH

Orgelbüchlein (*Little Organ Book*) (Nov., Vol. 13). Short arrangements of the chorales, some **E.**

Eight Short Preludes and Fugues (Nov.) some **E.**

The Larger Preludes and Fugues. It is impossible to list all of them, but the easier ones include the one in E Minor, and the little G Minor; despite difficulties an organist really should learn the Toccata and Fugue in D Minor sometime, and one day the great G Minor and the Passacaglia in C Minor (Nov.). This is a start.

Other suggested works by Bach:

Largo ma non Tanto (from Second Violin Concerto), arr. D. G. Murray (Nov.).

Air on the G String (from Suite in D), arr. J. S. Archer (Paxton).

Jesu, Joy of Man's Desiring, arr. Harvey Grace (O.U.P.).

The Organist's Bach (Paxton). Small, cheap edition.

Sheep May Safely Graze (O.U.P.) **E.**

HANDEL

Organ Concertos (some of the movements are not difficult). The arrangement by Dupré (Bornemann, Paris) incorporates the orchestral part into the texture, making the movements continuous, and playable on the organ alone.

Organ arrangements (two books, Nov.). Some of the many pieces are very **E.**

Other suggested works by Handel:

Arrival of the Queen of Sheba (*Solomon*), arr. J. S. Archer (Paxton).

The Water Music, arr. O. H. Peasgood (Nov.). Some movements **E.**

Minuet in G Minor, arr. R. W. Robson (Paxton).

Three Pieces from the *Music for the Royal Fireworks*, arr. Blake (O.U.P.).

COUPERIN

Soeur Monique, arr. G. Weitz (Nov.) **E.**

SCARLATTI

Pastorale (Harpsichord Sonata), arr. G. Beard (Nov.) **E.**

RAMEAU

Deux Ritornelles, arr. K. Elert (Paxton).

PURCELL

Trumpet Tunes and Ayres, arr. O. H. Peasgood (Nov.) **E.**

TARTINI

Aria in G, arr. J. S. Archer (Paxton) **E.**

STANLEY

Air in D Minor (Bos.) **E.**

Introduction and Allegro, arr. Coleman (Cramer).

W. BOYCE

Symphony No. 4 in F, arr. A. Hutchings (Nov.).

J. CLARKE

Trumpet Voluntary, arr. D. Ratcliff (Nov.) **E.**

FESTING

Largo, Allegro, Aria and Two Variations, arr. Thalben Ball (Nov.) **E.**

MOZART

Larghetto (Clarinet Concerto), arr. Best (Nov.).
Fantasia in F Minor (for a Mechanical Organ) (Nov.).
Minuet and Trio (Symphony No. 39) (Paxton-*Climax* Album).

ROMANTIC — VICTORIAN

ELGAR

Nimrod (*Enigma Variations*), arr. Harris (Nov.) **E.**

GRIEG

Triumphal March, Op. 65, No. 3, arr. R. Groves (Hin.—Peters edition).

RHEINBERGER

Sonatas in C Minor, No. 1, and E Minor, No. 8 (Nov.).

S. S. WESLEY

Three Short Pieces for Organ, ed. J. West (Nov.).

WIDOR

Symphony No. 5 (Hamelle—U.M.P.).

CÉSAR FRANCK

Chorale 3 in A Minor (Nov.).

EDWARDIAN

WALFORD DAVIES

Solemn Melody (Nov.) **E.**

MODERN

MESSIAEN

La Nativité du Seigneur (Leduc, Paris).

HINDEMITH

Sonatas Nos. 1 and 3 (Sch.).

Climax Albums for Organ (Paxton). Transcriptions — Bach, Beethoven, Boccherini, Brahms, Haydn, Mozart, Schumann, etc. Try Vols. 6 and 15 — some **E** works.

Funeral Album (Nov.): Handel, Chopin, Haydn, Mozart, Schumann, etc.

Wedding Music for Organ (Nov.): Mendelssohn, Wagner, etc.

Antologia per la Santa Messa, ed. Zanon (Ric.): thirty-five easy little pieces for manuals only, by J. S. Bach, Couperin, Frescobaldi, Vivaldi, etc. Ideal quiet pieces of quality.

SERIES

Modern Transcriptions for Organ (Nov.). Huge quantities of transcriptions by J. S. Archer, W. T. Best, J. West, etc.

This list of voluntaries offers only a few suggestions; it is not meant to be complete, nor does it include much twentieth-century organ music. But if anybody in a congregation thinks that organ music is dull, the organist has obviously not explored the field sufficiently; he should also make transcriptions of (non-copyright) music of which he is particularly fond. For example, the following pieces make admirable organ transcriptions:

Gluck, *Air of the Blessed Spirits* (Orpheus).
Beethoven, *Egmont* Overture: introductory bars.
Beethoven, *The Song of Rejoicing* (*Pastoral* Symphony).

When an organist has an adequate repertoire, he can put up a notice by the door of the church, giving the titles of the pieces to be played before and after the service. This serves a double purpose: (1) it helps the organist to decide what he is going to play, in advance — and thus the piece will get more practice, and (2) it interests the congregation in the organ and organ music. An organist might even have a complete list of his repertoire: it would help wedding couples to select music, and members of the choir or congregation could request special music on occasions, which they would know that the organist could play.

EXTEMPORISATION

Sometimes a piece comes to an end, and the choir can just be seen appearing in the chancel at the beginning of the service;

since it will be a full thirty seconds before they are in their places, and it is impossible to begin another piece, one must just keep going. This special art of extemporisation is yet another skill which an organist must have. At its worst it can be described as "filling in the silences"; if done well, choirboys have been known to ask their organist: "How is it your pieces always seem to end at exactly the right moment?"*

The subject is really too big for a book of this size, but we can offer a few suggestions. Extemporisation (which really equals composition) presupposes:

(1) A good grasp of harmony.
(2) A feeling for form.
(3) Some understanding of melody.
(4) Preferably a little knowledge of counterpoint.

With these four, one can do something. There are books on all these subjects—separately and together; but one really needs a teacher to correct exercises and give a little guidance as well. In many musical magazines there are advertisements: "F. Montague Butham, A.R.C.O., L.R.A.M., coaching for musical theory exams.—L.R.A.M., 1,432 successes; A.R.C.M., 2,194 successes; beginners also taken." If a man teaches from the beginning to L.R.A.M. standard, he needs to be a first-class musician, knowing his job from A to Z. Work hard under his guidance, but don't get swamped by too much paper-work, as extemporisation is a live art. In Germany, as part of the organ lesson, a pupil is given a chorale, or hymn tune (melody only), and is made to extemporise on it.

Here are some ways to keep extemporisation work alive and practical.

HARMONY

Practise arrangements of the four cadences (Perfect V I, Imperfect I V, Interrupted V VI, Plagal IV I) through all keys (Major and Minor) until they are familiar.

Precede these cadences by one chord (e.g. put IV before V, II before IV, etc.).

* An organist needs a sense of "timing"; for example, in the Church of England Eucharist, the priest must not be kept waiting for the music to stop when all the communicants have left the altar and he is ready to begin the Lord's Prayer.

Practise successions of chords with roots rising a fourth; roots falling a third, etc.

With one chord per bar, invent four-bar patterns, and make melodies to fit the harmony selected (e.g. I, V, V, I).

Vary the speed of the chord-change (one per bar, two per bar, etc.).

Fix all the above in the memory, until they become "harmonic schemes" on which one can base one's extemporisation.

FORM

Work first in schemes of three, playing with units, like bricks; AAB, ABA, ABB, ABC. These are the four basic schemes. A, B and C can be anything. Let A = a chord, B = a phrase of a melody, C = five descending notes. Later these units can be bigger. Let A = a succession of four chords, B = a phrase of a melody, with accompaniment, C = an arpeggio up and down. Equally well, A can be a four-bar melody, B can be arpeggios, C can be scales. Eventually A = a section of sixteen bars, B = a contrasting section of twelve bars, etc. Try always to make sense with the ingredients—not just unrelated fragments (see examples given below).

(1)

In an example such as (1), most people would feel that the third bar needed some variation. (Not always! Many of the great composers dare to repeat a phrase exactly!) In example (2) (ABB2) the third section is directly related to the second, but varies the material.

(2)

One should now try AA2B: ABA2: ABB2.

Next, one can work in schemes of four: AAAB; AABA; ABAA; ABBB, etc.; the idea is to think in units, and gradually to enlarge these.

Examine other composers: start with very simple compositions (e.g. easy songs, German dances, hymns, etc.).

MELODY

Practise "Question and Answer" method: two bars are given — reply with two of your own (make several attempts).

Choose four short melodies which are personal favourites, and make graphs of their contours (rise and fall). Examine the shapes of the "waves of sound" quite analytically — look for the climax, and for sequences, at the endings of each phrase (compare them) — examine for modulations, special rhythmic features, and try to discover what the real success of each tune is due to.

At the organ (or piano) invent your own melodies, concentrating on one point at a time: e.g. (1) a scheme of modulation, (2) good contours, (3) rhythmic features, etc.

Gradually try to combine two points — e.g. modulation and contours, or contours and rhythm; these melodies should not be accompanied at all at first.

COUNTERPOINT

There can be few better extemporisation disciplines than strict counterpoint.

(1) Play the given tune (say, a hymn) with the right hand (in strict rhythm, but very slowly at first); play a second part that goes with it note by note, using concords only (unison, third, (fourth*), fifth, sixth, octave) in the left hand. Try to prefer contrary motion (the two hands going in opposite directions) to similar motion — it gives the parts independence. You can be

---

* Fourth—considered a discord by older composers. Compared against the fifth it is a little difficult to understand this.

"academic" and avoid consecutive fifths and octaves (i.e. two fifths or two octaves, one after another), or you can deliberately be "unacademic" and have consecutive fifths, etc., on purpose. But it is important to do this on purpose, and not by mistake.

Then reverse — tune in the left hand, counterpoint in the right. This method in Palestrina style is called *First Species*.

(2) Now to every note of the tune, the other hand plays two notes of equal value; otherwise everything applies as before. Reverse as before. This is called *Second Species*.

(The numbers between the staves (see example) show the "intervals" between the two hands. Every effort has been made in these examples to keep to concords. One should be listening all the time as one plays. Discords are allowed — academically — as passing notes, and as sevenths which are resolved; but this is getting beyond the scope of this book.)

All the above must be played *in time*. As this is not easy at first, it is advisable to choose a *very slow beat*.

As we live in the twentieth century, when ideas on concord and discord are changing rapidly, it is suggested, for interest, that one repeats the above two exercises (as soon as one has mastered them in the first manner on several hymns), (*a*) with alternating concord and discord (try to make the second part a good melody), and (*b*) with discords only (2nd (4th), Aug. 4th, 7th); this is much more difficult as there are so few discords available. Counterpoint means the controlled combining of melodies — the control is partly by means of the interval between the melodies. Counterpoin should therefore explore all intervals (not just concords).

In all the above, one should be (*a*) experimenting, but (*b*) trying to hear what is going to be played slightly in advance, so that concords and discords come as planned, and do not take one by surprise.

(3) *Third Species*. Three or four (or more) notes to one.

(4) *Fourth Species*. Suspensions.

(5) *Fifth Species*. A combination of the above methods.

These last three methods need considerable amplification, but this is beyond the scope of this book. A teacher must help here; in the fifth species, where more choice is available, the harmony should sound natural (not necessarily commonplace), and the rhythm should flow along easily.

These four elements can now be combined gradually, and quite methodically. Harmony and form; melody and form (without harmony); counterpoint and harmony, etc. When all four elements are combined, one is in fact composing or, rather, extemporising. Most of the elements must be subconscious, or "second nature", otherwise the whole process would proceed in jerks — but this is only to say that a carpenter, when he is making a chest, must be able to plane by instinct, with a natural understanding of the grain of the wood; at the same time he must understand the form or shape of the finished piece of furniture (otherwise it is put together in the wrong order); he needs specialised knowledge of grooves, glueing, etc. In fact it takes time and perseverance to make a good carpenter, and a good extemporiser — both are relatively rare.

While the process is developing, however, here is a very simple little scheme for "extemporising" quietly, which can be used in sections — employing whatever section one wishes in any particular order. It is based on a simple hymn tune, and uses the theme and variations form.

(1) Play the hymn as written.

(2) Second species counterpoint — tune in the right hand, counterpoint in the left hand — have nice fresh stops, and allow yourself freedom (i.e. break the rigorous second species) with each cadence.

(3) Repeat the hymn with different harmonies, or possibly with the same harmonies in another octave (higher or lower). Hands on the same manual.

(4) Repeat (2) with the hands reversed.

106

(5) Now take a distinctive feature of the hymn (e.g. the first four notes), and instead of continuing with the tune, repeat it sequentially and develop it. Continue to have resting (or cadence) points. The harmonies could be in the other hand, and at half the pace (i.e. if the hymn is generally in crotchets, the chords will be in minims). Again, break the scheme slightly at cadence points.

(6) Conclude with the hymn.

A few points on the above:

(a) The key-system as it stands will be a little tedious; if the organist can transpose, sections (2) and (4) could be in another key—say the dominant or subdominant (transposition is considered later in this chapter).

(b) Further interest could be added by changing the mode—major, minor, and vice versa.

(c) As the organist becomes better at three notes, four notes, six notes (? five) to one (third species), the second and fourth sections can become more varied and interesting.

(d) Further variations can be made by alternating harmony and counterpoint (first line harmony, second line counterpoint), provided the idea is carried through.

(e) The organ is an excellent instrument for inserting "echo-ideas" which can break the regular form of the hymn.

(f) As fresh ideas of construction occur, jot them down, so that they can be used again. This is only a start.

At first an organist may prefer to write his extemporisations down. This will enable him to get over the business of transposing, and give him a little more confidence. A word of advice: "a journey of a thousand miles begins with one step" (Chinese proverb).

ACCOMPANIMENT

As well as being a performer and extemporiser, an organist must also be a good accompanist. In a sense, an organist accompanies hymns and psalms, but in another sense he also leads. A congregation (or a weak choir, for that matter) cannot be relied upon to keep the beat going, and therefore the organist is responsible for the timing in its two aspects—rhythm and pulse. A good accompanist is, in fact, both a sensitive follower and an assertive leader; the degree in which he is one or the other depends on his partner. The situation can be seen quite clearly if one tabulates it:

(1) *Organist with a good pulse* plays with *partner whose rhythm is weak*, e.g. a congregation, a weak choir, a dragging singer, etc. Organist senses the weakness immediately, and takes control. If the organ speaks late in addition (which it usually does), his degree of assertion has to be very pronounced. Rhythm can be helped by degrees of *staccato*.

(2) *Organist with a good pulse* plays with *partner whose rhythm is good*. Organist shares the responsibility for the beat.

(3) *Organist with a good pulse* plays with *partner whose rhythm is outstandingly good*. Organist can be mainly subservient (and it is a pleasure to be so); this is what some people mean when they think of accompanying. It only happens very rarely with a first-class musician.

(4) *Organist with a bad pulse* plays with *partner whose rhythm is weak*. Both sides get slower and slower. Anybody who is musical finds he can bear it no longer.

(5) *Organist with a bad pulse* plays with a *partner whose rhythm is good*. The soloist realises the trouble, and pulls the organist along if possible (this is possible so long as the organ is not too loud).

(6) *Organist with a bad pulse* plays with *partner whose rhythm is outstandingly good*. The soloist either inspires the organist to do some work, showing quite remarkable patience; or the two part company.

This only goes to show that an organist must, above all, have a good sense of rhythm. If he hasn't this by nature, it can be achieved by work. This is so important (in (4) above people are being driven away from the church service) that a few words will not be out of place on how to improve one's sense of rhythm.

(*a*) Use scales or arpeggios as a foundation. Work out quite straightforward rhythms with ♩ and ♩ (e.g. ♩ ♩♩), and see four octaves of scales or arpeggios through on this rhythm. Initially ♩ = 120, but eventually ♩ = 480. Now invent rhythms with ♪, ♩ and ♩ (e.g. ♩ ♫♩ or ♫♩ ♩ ♩ etc.). Finally use ♪,♪, ♩ and ♩ (e.g. ♩ ♬♬♫ ♩).

(*b*) Hindemith has whole lists of exercises in two parts in his *Elementary Training for Musicians* (Sch.). The basic idea is to play one rhythm and tap another; both rhythms are of course obeying the same pulse as in the example below.

e.g. *Play* (on one note)

Foot

If this seems too easy, reverse the foot and hands. Exercises of this sort can be devised by anybody, and the principle can be stretched as one likes (e.g. three rhythms – RH, LH and Foot).

(*c*) Now play hymns with the hands only, stamping out the beat with the foot. Then stamp with the other foot.

(*d*) Collect a member of the choir and ask him to sing a hymn, dragging deliberately. Force him to sing in time by playing with a good pulse.

By methods of this kind it is possible slowly to toughen up one's rhythm; but it is a long process.

Although an organist needs a very good sense of pulse (rhythm is one of his chief expressive powers), he must not become the absolute slave of this sense. Phrasing may demand slight relaxation of the beat. A very common example can be found in hymns, at the end of a line. Sometimes a line ends with two or more beats; there is then ample time to breathe but, if there is only one beat, it may be necessary to allow the choir and congregation extra breathing space. If the organist breathes himself, he will know instinctively how much time to give. This same art applies to all music; it is one of the things that breaks the mechanical stiffness of the rhythm. Hymn books sometimes place commas at these points (e.g. in tunes like *Nativity*, *Bishopthorpe* (from lines 2–3)); examples are very numerous.

TRANSPOSITION

This is another useful art. Hymns occasionally lie too high for a congregation, and should be brought down. Generally D is about the limit, but the occasional E flat and E natural are all right, provided they are not sustained notes. (This is not an absolute rule – when a congregation is large and excited, the men may even reach F without realising it.) High notes are partly psychological; when a tune is known, the high notes are taken more easily. It is advisable at practices for the choirmaster to transpose down some higher passages until they are learnt. A transposed edition of *Hymns Ancient and Modern* is published (see page 53).

Transposition has three sides: (1) the harmonic side, (2) the solfa side, (3) a technical side.

Let us take the harmonic side first. If an organist can look at a hymn and say immediately "That is chord I, root position, followed by chord VI, root position, etc.", the chords are easily transposed to another key. Instead of analysing single notes, he is working in units. Coupled with this ability, an experienced organist hears the two chords in his mind, and reproduces this progression in another key almost by second nature. The reason is that he has played this progression of chords so many thousand times that he *knows it* by sound and feel in a certain number of the commoner keys.

The solfa side develops in the process of transferring solfa to staff notation. A child can sing *doh, mi, soh, la*. In the key of C this is C, E, G, A; in the key of E it is E, G sharp, B, C sharp; in the key of B flat it is B flat, D, F, G. A good transposer looks at a melody in G major and says "this is G, A, C, B, or *doh, ray, fah, me. Doh, ray, fah, me* in another key would be . . ." Most of this is obvious enough; however, if one is transposing Hindemith, for example, one may forget about this side, but it still exists.

The technical side is purely mechanical. Transposition up or down one—everything on a line moves into a space, everything in a space moves on to a line. This is partly a trick of the eye, like seeing slightly crooked. This skill is the most valuable of all the transposition skills; a singer usually wants a song down one, a hymn usually goes down one, trumpets and clarinets in B flat go down one, etc. Semitone or tone needs differentiating, of course.

Another way to transpose up or down is to change the key-signature and alter the accidentals; this is not always as easy as it sounds, and is a slightly different skill to the other methods (where line becomes space, etc.), but it is perfectly acceptable as a method. When transposing up or down a tone, white becomes white, black becomes black, except over the gap between the black keys. Thus, when transposing up a tone, G becomes A, and G sharp becomes A sharp; but B becomes C sharp, and E becomes

F sharp. Similarly, when transposing down a tone, D becomes C, and E flat becomes D flat; but F becomes E flat, and C becomes B flat.

Books are quite unnecessary to develop this skill. Every choir practice, one can move lines up or down. "Tenors, let's try that a semitone higher." One learns a hymn down a tone, and plays it that way on Sunday, if necessary writing it out at first to give confidence. One of the present writers practised his transposition first on hymns, and later on Haydn sonatas and the Bach "48". The more one does, the greater the degree of confidence.

Transposition up or down a third. Spaces and lines move up or down to the next space or line. One can give oneself practice with a friend. He calls out "C"; one immediately plays "A" (transposing down a third). F = D; B = G, and so forth. This increases one's speed of response. This method can be used also with chords, cadences, etc. The friend says "C", and one plays a perfect cadence in A; he says "G", and one plays a first inversion of the chord of E — and so on.

There are little tricks with clefs which some people find useful and some examples are given below.

If one knows the tenor clef as well, more tricks can be worked out.

Transposing down a third in 𝄢: Turn 𝄢 into 𝄞 (and adjust to the right octave)

Transposing up a third in 𝄞 Turn 𝄞 into 𝄢:

Transposing up a second in 𝄞 Turn 𝄞 into 𝄡 (alto)

TRAINING AND APPOINTMENTS

An organist usually begins as a pianist (as we have said earlier in this chapter), and starts the organ after reaching about the level of Grade V (Associated Board). He may then study privately, perhaps measuring his progress by taking some of the Associated Board's examinations in Organ Playing (Grades IV to VIII). Or he may go to one of the main music colleges, or to The Royal School of Church Music, where the course may last three years or more; at the end of this he may take one of the examinations of the Royal College of Organists. He usually finds a job (1) through answering advertisements in musical journals, or in the music colleges, or (2) through personal connections in his own home district or outside. An organist who is an exceptionally fine performer may manage, without his church appointment,* as a recital organist. But such people are very rare. The normal organist is a man of considerable musicianship, as performer, accompanist, extemporiser and transposer (his other side as choirmaster being kept for the next chapter) — and these skills require constant practice, or they may fall into disuse. The call on his time is in fact enormous. It may seem unfair to add a criticism when there is so much that is "positive" in a church organist, but it would be unbalanced to omit it. This is due (1) to the very nature of Church music, buried deep in the past, (2) to the constant pre-occupation with a regular pulse, (3) to the mechanical nature of the organ, and (4) to the huge number of calls on his time. At his worst, an organist can be unadventurous in taste, rhythmically stiff, unaware of other music, and unwilling to change his ways. At his best, an organist can be a man of great musicianship, very varied skills, an open mind and a generous disposition.

THE ROYAL COLLEGE OF ORGANISTS

Membership of the Royal College of Organists (founded in 1864) is open "to all who take an interest in the work and profession of the Organist, as well as those desirous of gaining the Diplomas of the College". Members may attend all the organ recitals, concerts, and the valuable lectures on organ playing, choir training, etc., which are given by the College; they may also make use of the College library, and may use the College organ for private practice on payment of a small fee.

Examinations in organ playing are held in January and July at the College in London, and in January at Glasgow. The practical requirements of the examination for the Diploma of Associate (A.R.C.O.) are the performance of two compositions for the organ; the playing at sight of a passage of organ music on three staves;

---

* A suggested scale of salaries for five categories of (C. of E.) organist's posts will be found in *English Church Music* (R.S.C.M., 1964). Also included is "An Enquiry into the Appointment of Organists and Choirmasters in Ten English Dioceses", giving replies to a questionnaire on duties, composition of choirs, remuneration, etc.

the playing from a four-part vocal score (three parts in the G clef and one in the F clef); and the transposition of a hymn tune up or down a tone or semitone. Paper-work comprises the harmonisation of a chorale-melody for four voices in the style of Bach; the addition of not more than three parts to a given part, using the harmonic idiom of the Haydn–Mozart period; questions on the history of English Church music; the writing of a piece of two-part counterpoint in the style of Bach; and three-part counterpoint for keyboard and strings.

For the Fellowship examination (F.R.C.O.) the practical work requires a higher standard of playing, and the ability to harmonise a melody and extemporise. The paper-work includes the writing of a passage in eighteenth or early nineteenth century style; the writing of an instrumental fugal exposition on a given subject in three parts; the writing of a short chorale prelude for organ on a given theme, or the addition of two parts to a given part in the style of Palestrina; also questions on general musical history of a given period.

Seven prizes and a Silver Medal are awarded upon the results of the Diploma examinations, and there are several scholarships and exhibitions tenable at the Royal Academy of Music, the Royal College of Music, etc., with organ playing as the principal study.

There are two choir training examinations which are held once a year in May. The "Certificate" examination, in which successful candidates receive a certificate but do not have the right to append any letters to their name, consists of (1) paper-work, with questions on the formation and training of choirs, the teaching of the rudiments of music, psalm and hymn singing (Anglican and plainsong), and general knowledge of Church music, and (2) a practical section in which the candidate must be prepared to rehearse a small choir (SATB) which will be in attendance, and to accompany on the organ a hymn, psalm or anthem; also to answer questions arising out of these tests.

The "Diploma" choir training examination is open to Fellows or Associates; successful candidates are entitled to append the letters CHM (Choir Master) to their Diploma designation thus: F.R.C.O. (CHM) or A.R.C.O. (CHM). Like the "Certificate" examination there are two sections: (1) paper-work, and (2) practical and viva voce, but a higher standard is required in each section.

A list of selected books on various aspects of Church music will be found in the bibliography; in addition, there are numerous small books and pamphlets of interest to organists and church musicians.

The "Occasional and Shorter Papers" published at very modest prices by the Church Music Society (obtainable from O.U.P.) cover many aspects of Church music such as *Music of the Holy Communion* (J. H. Arnold), *Restoration Church Music* (Heathcote Statham), *The Use of Small Church Organs* (S. H. Lovett), and *Congregational Hymn Practices* (C. E. Daly), to name but a few of these valuable papers. A recent publication is *A Repertory of English Cathedral Anthems*, compiled by John Dykes Bower and Allan Wicks.

The "Study Notes" published by the R.S.C.M. are concise essays on practical subjects, with books recommended for further study, where appropriate. The twelve books in this series include *Chanting for Beginners* (Hubert Crook), *Choir Training* (Dr. Percy Saunders), *Hymn Tunes — an Historical Outline* (Dr. Erik Routley), and *Plainsong Hymns and Sequences* (Denis Stevens). Also published by the R.S.C.M. are six "Lists of Recommended Music": (1) *Church Music* — a graded list recommended by the Musical Advisory Board of the R.S.C.M.; (2) *Pianoforte Voluntaries* (for use in schools); (3) *Music for Treble Voices*; (4) *Carols for Christmas, Epiphany and Easter;* (5) *Easy Organ Voluntaries*; (6) *Recordings of English Choral Music.* Another small but valuable book published by the R.S.C.M. is a statement by its founder (Sir Sydney Nicholson) of the institution's *Principles and Recommendations* (at Morning and Evening Prayer, Holy Communion, etc.).

The ideals of Anglican Church music are set out in two reports by the Archbishops' Committee; the first *Music in Worship* (S.P.C.K., 1922–1947), and the second *Music in Church* (Church Information Office, 1951 — revised 1960). The Church Information Office also publishes notes on *Organists in Parish Churches* (setting out the duties, etc., of organist and choirmaster), *Music in Children's Worship*, and *Organs and Organ Cases for Parish Churches.*

The National Federation of Music Societies, 4 St. James's Square, London, S.W.1, publish a booklet on *Choral Latin*, which gives guidance in pronunciation for choirs who sing the Mass, the Requiem Mass, and the *Stabat Mater* in Latin.

CHAPTER SIX

THE CHOIR AND ITS CHOIRMASTER

The previous chapter dealt with the many varied tasks which an organist is called upon to perform. The job of choirmaster is in many ways completely different, but in most of the churches of this country it is undertaken by the same man. While an organist could be an introvert, the choirmaster's job demands a more extroverted type. Small wonder, then, that under the strain organists-cum-choirmasters sometimes develop remarkable and strange personalities!

A choirmaster needs to be (1) teacher, (2) disciplinarian, (3) musician with a sensitive ear for pitch, vocal tone, diction, etc., (4) Christian; and his job is easier if he has (5) a good or reasonable voice, (6) ability to get on well with the other authorities within the church, (7) a constant flow of fresh ideas, (8) social gifts, and (9) the power of self-criticism.

As there are so many requirements, it would be understandable if few musicians attempted this enormous job (especially as it is usually underpaid, and sometimes unpaid); but the opposite is in fact the case. If one is a Christian it represents an idealistic job at the very centre of one's faith. It is usually a job "across the classes" —all can sing and be loyal to a group. The job gives access to a fine instrument (the organ); and the possibility of good performance from the enormous choral repertoire, as well as from hymns and psalms, is an exciting prospect. But a period as assistant organist (cum-accompanist) is advisable, so that one can gain from the experience of another organist. The other method of learning—trial, error and success—takes longer, though it may produce in the end a more vital man. Given the will to learn, every single qualification listed above can be acquired and improved upon (even self-criticism!).

AS TEACHER

This means that it is no use being a first-rate musician unless one can analyse the ingredients and put them across in assimilable doses. Every child should be taught to read music as well as to sing by imitation, and part of each practice (at least two a week) should be devoted to learning how to read. In this way a child develops a love of music—*and* skill. Here are a few hints (not particularly original ones).

Pitch. The aim is to make children concentrate on the "up-and-downness" of the notes. (1) Tell them to put a finger (clean!) below the note, and follow along as each note is played (or played and sung). (2) Instead of singing *La*, sing *Up*, *Down* or *Same* for each note. (3) Sing *La*, follow with the finger of one hand —with the other hand point *Up*, *Down* or *Level*. This is one way of starting off the process of reading; it can be done for a short time while learning a new tune, anthem or chant. Solfa gives a more exact method of pitching, but it must be connected with staff notation. After the relationships *Doh–Me–Soh* (for example) have been learnt, they must be repeated on the stave: line, next line up, next line up. *Doh–Fah* = line to next space up but one. Kodály, who has achieved such success with the reading of music by young children, swears by solmisation* (*Let us sing correctly* (B. & H.)), and he has several suggestions concerning intonation and the pentatonic scale† which should be helpful. The biggest obstacle to pitch is often the choirmaster himself. If he has been brought up as a pianist, he may have a weak sense of relative pitch. If so he should give himself dozens of exercises, turning simple hymn tunes, etc. (all four parts) into solfa and back again. He should sing one part of *Messiah* and play another on the piano (slowly, of course). The process may take several years, but at the end the sense of achievement, and the ability to "put it across" better to the child mind will repay every minute of work.

"But the adults? . . . They're worse than the children . . . They can't pitch at all." If an adult is quite unteachable, it is probably better for him to leave the choir; but this is really a failure in "putting it across". "Gentlemen of the basses, you are singing C, F. It should be C, G." What bass would walk out over such a comment? Every single practice should mean that a few more notes can be improved—over the years, they add up!

Rhythm. A choirmaster with a good rhythmic sense can easily

---

* *Solmisation:* sight-singing from staff notation, using solfa syllables as names of notes.
† *Pentatonic Scale:* a "gapped" scale with only five different notes to the octave; common to many ancient nations, and also characteristic of many old Scottish tunes. The scale may be represented by the black keys of the piano.

forget how difficult it is to think of two things at the same time (rhythm and pitch) — when they are both new and unmastered. It is often a good idea to isolate rhythmic problems from pitch problems, temporarily. "Will you please speak — without singing — 'Lea-ead me-ee Lor-or-ord'."

When a musician has a good sense of rhythm, he feels the pulse and subdivides the beat as a matter of habit. This habit can be acquired by almost everybody, provided they persist long enough. The solfa method is excellent. There is another more mathematical method which can also be used:

(a) ♩ = 1: 𝅗𝅥 = 1, 2: 𝅗𝅥. = 1, 2, 3: ♫ = ½ ½.

Sections of anthems, etc. can be practised by counting the rhythm out. Later the notes can be sung at the right pitch, singing with numbers. Children can stamp with their feet as they sing, to feel the pulse more strongly. Methods can be devised for other rhythms as in (b),

(b) ♩. ♪ = "1 and a dot ½"

the word "dot" occurring exactly on the second beat. These rhythms need driving deep into everybody's system. Words with natural rhythms

(c) ♫♪ = holiday, ♫ = choirboy, ♫. = Britten

are useful. In rhythm it must be remembered that there are *two* things to reach — rhythm (or the subdivisions of the beat) and the maintenance of the pulse itself.

The other points to do with reading music — e.g. expression, feeling for phrase, dynamics, etc. — though each in its way absolutely vital, are secondary to the basic questions of rhythm and pitch.

AS DISCIPLINARIAN

The job becomes easier in so far as the choirmaster improves his discipline. A very few choirmasters have natural discipline; the majority have to learn by bitter trial and error. If the choirmaster is not a natural disciplinarian, however, the practice goes better if it has been worked out beforehand. If the minister chooses the hymns, the choirmaster is entitled to insist on having them a week in advance. If the organist chooses the hymns, it is a good idea to have all details of psalms, hymns, chants and anthems worked out a month (or more) ahead. A few rules of a very simple nature can be invented — "As soon as I play the first chord on the piano, there is to be no more talking." When Smith talks he is mercilessly thrown out for a week. "Ah. But . . ." pleads the harassed choirmaster, "I have only six boys. I can't afford . . ." Try it and see. The boy will be back at the first opportunity. One more hint: work very fast, and move from one item to the next so quickly that there is little time for misbehaviour. If the choir is very slow at finding their places — "First boy to find hymn twenty-seven stand up. Good, Smith — one conduct point." There is no detail too piffling for a choirmaster to try to solve — think of Christ washing the feet of His disciples.

AS SENSITIVE MUSICIAN

A choirmaster should never be satisfied with his own abilities. There is never a time when he is entitled to stop trying.

AS A CHRISTIAN

This colours everything the choirmaster does — and gives him a sense of purpose. It also enables him to work with and under other people. But please — a pious choirmaster who is an amateur theologian . . .

IF HE HAS A REASONABLE VOICE

There are a great many good choirmasters with no voice of their own — certainly many with a voice one would not wish to copy. But one of the finest living choirmasters has a wonderful voice, and is able to illustrate immediately how he wants a phrase to be sung — also how not to sing it (roars of laughter). No good piano teacher would dare to teach the piano unless he could play reasonably well himself. If a choirmaster has a poor voice, he should put himself under a good singing teacher, and humbly submit to the ordeal. He will find himself remarkably stupid (in the eyes of the teacher); remarkably bad at co-ordinating breathing apparatus, lips, jaw, tongue; completely unable at first to "place" his voice anywhere different from where it is at present. But this humiliating experience can do him nothing but good. A warning though — singing teachers are not all good; it may take a little time (and some tactful enquiries) to find a teacher who understands his pupil's troubles, and who is able to deal with them correctly.

IF HE HAS ABILITIES TO GET ON WITH THE OTHER
AUTHORITIES IN THE CHURCH

This very tricky problem is touched on in Chapter Eight.

IF HE HAS A CONSTANT FLOW OF FRESH IDEAS

Some choirmasters are quite happy with the "routine music" of the Church services (hymns, psalms, anthems, etc.). But some members, teenagers especially, require constant excitement, and something on which to test their newly-developed musical skills (the other skills are not necessarily the concern of the choirmaster!). There are small cantatas, with organ only, or with a quartet of strings, or anthems with one *obbligato* instrument. There are older works for choir and four trombones, and other brass instruments. There are special "Festival days"—Good Friday, Easter, Christmas, Patronal Festival, Ascension Day—and each occasion can be marked with special music. Besides these there are the great works, and if one's choir is too small to perform a work like the St. John Passion of J. S. Bach—in combination with other choirs all sorts of things are possible. A work once learnt in combination with other choirs can be performed in more than one church. A church choir can enter for competitive or non-competitive festivals, and can be visited by a "Special Commissioner" from the Royal School of Church Music. Suggestions for music are included in Chapter Seven. What about a small concert given by talented choir members?

IF HE HAS SOCIAL GIFTS

A choirmaster may not have enough time to devote to this side of the choir. But younger people are usually happier if there are further non-musical activities attached to a choir; e.g. table tennis after the practice; cricket matches for the boys against other churches; a summer outing to the coast; a Christmas outing (not always to some traditional entertainment); there are good operas which a choir can enjoy—and concerts—as well as circus and pantomime visits.

IF HE HAS THE GIFT OF SELF-CRITICISM

A choirmaster can become a little dictator, who is gradually impervious to all forms of criticism from outside. His own organ playing can get steadily worse, and the choir equally difficult and unmusical in its performance. There are very few vicars who dare to get rid of an organist who has been in the same job for twenty years. However bad he is, the internal ramifications of "church life" are such that bold moves of this sort carry repercussions for years to come. However good a choirmaster is, he can always be better. If he cannot believe it, let him listen to some records of first-rate performances, and compare them against his own choir. If he regards his own situation as unique ("the difficulties are insuperable here"), let him visit another church with virtually the same set-up and see if he finds anything better there.

So much for the choirmaster himself. A few general hints on choir training may be acceptable at this point.

HYMNS

Every Sunday a great many hymns are sung (three services can mean thirteen hymns). Therefore it is impossible to practice all the hymns thoroughly. One method is to select one (or two) hymns for extra treatment; for all the rest, sing through one selected verse confidently. If confidence is lacking, that particular hymn can be changed for another better-known tune, or for another hymn altogether, or more time can be spent on that hymn at the expense of some other part of the practice.

THE HYMNS SELECTED FOR EXTRA REHEARSAL

(1) Are the notes right in each part? Three-quarters of the choir must sit still while the particular part is practised. It may not be possible to get 100 per cent in one practice; if this is so, the choirmaster should make a mental note for the next occasion the hymn turns up.

(2) Is the rhythm secure? One note may be two beats long: there may be a dotted rhythm which is insufficiently alert (e.g. "Jesus shall reign"—tune *Truro*). Are quavers slurred over? The first quaver of a pair of slurred quavers tends to be sung too fast (e.g. "As pants the hart for cooling streams"—tune *Martyrdom*).

(3) Unanimity of attack. There should be a recognised scheme between the organist's play-over of the tune, and the start of the hymn. For this reason, the organist must perform his play-over in very good rhythm, taking off the last note exactly as planned with the choir. The length of the last notes of each line need practising

to secure good attack on the next line; if there is no break in the rhythm between the lines (e.g. Bach chorales, and lines three to four of "Teach me my God and King"—tune *Sandys*), will the organist make a slight break, or will he carry straight through? Does the choir start immediately the organ plays, or does it wait one beat? There are good arguments for different solutions to these problems, but the choirmaster needs to plan his particular solution, and stick to it until it succeeds.

(4) If the above points are good, and the choir sings with confident tone and in tune, then is the time to work at the style of the hymn. *A plainsong-type hymn* requires a steady flow of *legato* tone. Avoid "bashing" each note—select words which require natural speech stress, and give these notes a little extra; the best way to do this is to emphasise the actual vowel sound of the stressed word, possibly giving the initial consonant a slight extra attack. If this overdoes the required effect, the excess can always be removed by smoothing it out. For example, "O come, O come, Emmanuel"— tune *Veni Emmanuel*: stress the vowels in "come" both times (is it really "u" as in "but"?); the syllable "ma" (of "Emmanuel") should also receive stress, with the lips coming together lightly for the initial "m". If this produces a bumpy sound-wave the choirmaster, by imitation, can smooth out the total effect in an instant. The overall flow should go fast enough (*a*) not to leave the congregation behind, and (*b*) to get a sentence in easily in one breath. A *missionary-type hymn* needs, on the contrary, a very good and pronounced rhythm. This can, however, produce the terrible "plod-plod" effect which often makes church choirs a laughing-stock outside the church; a judicious admixture of *legato* (i.e. *legato* plus *marcato*) is the solution to this. If "Onward, Christian soldiers" —tune *St. Gertrude*—produces a sound-wave like the one shown in the example (*a*), it should be practised slowly in an effort to produce a more even sound, as in (*b*).

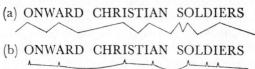

(a) ONWARD CHRISTIAN SOLDIERS

(b) ONWARD CHRISTIAN SOLDIERS

That is to say, each note begins with a little *fp*—the vowel sound (*mf* not *f*) continues on towards the next sound. Practise this slowly on the right notes, first with vowels only (see (*c*) below).

Insist on continuity of sound, with only one breath, then add consonants at the end of each vowel (no anticipating) as in (*d*). Finally, for the dramatic sense, add a little extra stress to *CHRI* and *SOL*.

(c) Vowels only   Ŏ ER Ĭ ER OH OH ER

(d) Ŏ - nwER - dkrĬ - styER - nsOH - OH - ldyER - z

After one or two lines have been practised like this, the choir may get the overall idea. *Most other hymns* fall between these two extreme types so that, provided the choir can sing "O come, O come, Emmanuel" and "Onward Christian soldiers" with a real sense of style, the hymn singing of the choir is "on the move".

(5) *In unison hymns* the following things are important: (*a*) a long note—is it part of a *crescendo*, or a *diminuendo*? Long notes should never stand still (e.g. *Jerusalem*; "And did those feet"; "feet" should be *crescendoing* towards "in *an*cient time"); (*b*) where are the breaths to be taken? The choir needs to feel how long the phrases actually are; (*c*) the climax point of the tune (or possibly the words)—the whole choir should makes towards it; (*d*) basses in particular may get tired by constant singing of the melody, and a long unison hymn may gain by having some verses sung alternately—lower voices—upper voices.

PSALMS

(1) Learn the notes of the chant very thoroughly. A lot of bad psalm singing is due to the fact that the individual parts do not know their next notes.

(2) Some children cannot read words fast enough, especially difficult ones. This is one reason why children need the practice on their own.

(3) Does the whole choir really understand an Anglican chant? Under the pretence of teaching the children, the adults can be reminded of the basic principles. A single chant consists of two halves. Each half contains a reciting note and an ending note—in between are the "notes between the bar-lines" (this ties up historically with the plainsong from which the Anglican chant derives). The first half has two notes between the bar-lines, the second half four notes between two pairs of bar-lines.

Half
way

Reciting Note	Two notes between bar-lines	Ending Note	Reciting Note	Four notes between bar-lines	Ending Note
1	2 3	4	1	2 3 4 5	6

These notes can be given numbers 1–4 and 1–6. This helps to pinpoint any particular note which may be going wrong.

(4) The first problem is to get the choir to change the notes on exactly the right words. One method is to speak the words, stamping on the words where the note changes. When singing, some people still "can't get off the first note". One can stamp and point up or down; these are aids to concentration.

(5) Another problem is to sing the words steadily (without dragging or rushing) on the reciting note. If a choir has got into bad habits, an entirely mechanical way of achieving this is to sing every syllable of equal length. Then add the stresses (see page 121 under *plainsong-type hymns*); finally relax the exactness of the note-values, until the psalm achieves an even flow.

(6) Another problem is to proceed from note one to note two without dragging back. The origin of this was when there was a "gathering-note" in the *Cathedral Psalter*, when the choir deliberately stopped and waited for the congregation before proceeding to note two. Today, with the accent on speech-rhythm, this is considered unnatural.

(7) Some choirs hold on to the ending-note too long. The choir has difficulty in getting started on the next verse, and the whole psalm becomes too dragged out.

(8) Psalms flow best when the voice is "in the head" (i.e. not heavy "in the throat"), and they should not be sung too loudly. On the other hand, if the congregation is expected to sing, the choir should not sing too softly — this gives the congregation an inferiority complex.

(9) Notes between the bar-lines: when there are two syllables and two notes, all is easy; when there are three syllables, two syllables

go to one note, one to the other. Care should then be taken that these are sung as a triplet, as shown below, ♩♩♪ or ♪♩♩ (with triplet-3 markings) (not ♫♪ or ♪♫): where the first example achieves a better flow.

(10) Psalms can be sung to plainchant, and there is an "intermediate stage"—the Gélineau psalms. Except for different points where the notes change, the technique is not basically different.

(11) The different psalters, methods of pointing, etc., have been discussed in Chapter Two.

(12) It is interesting how the Anglican Church still insists on the regular use of the Psalms of David. To many the antiquated language and unfamiliar geography, etc., will appear irrelevant today. One of the jobs of a lively choirmaster is to bring these psalms up-to-date. To summarise, for instance, Psalm 44: 1–4 Our parents told us You were a powerful God (5–9) we will praise You for ever—even though (10–17) our enemies seem to be getting the better of us (18–22) we still have faith in You (23–26). You must have forgotten all about us. This is typical of a state of spiritual dryness—God's schemes are on a bigger scale—as we live from day to day, there are times when we feel He has deserted us.

ANTHEMS

The main difference here is that the choir is not leading the congregation, and hence it can make full use of the range of dynamics *pp–ff*. If there is an assistant organist, or if the choir can sing unaccompanied, it is much better that the choir should be conducted. If members of the congregation object to the element of display, they can be asked if they like their music well or merely indifferently sung. Unconducted music can also tend to be a little metronomic and stiff. There is quite an effective compromise where one member in the back pew of each side waves a finger up and down, followed minutely by the facing side. Choristers should hold their music up well, if the pews are not perfectly designed. Of course, if the choir were in a gallery at the back, as many feel it should be (so that (1) the singing is led from behind, (2) there is a clear view of the altar, and (3) the inevitable fidgety choirboys are out of sight), the problem of conducting would not come under question. A choir which has a large repertoire of anthems is a successful choir, and is bound to stay together (other things being equal). Also, for many choristers, the whole world of music may first be opened in the church pew: it is a big responsibility for the choirmaster.

There are a few general points of choir training which apply to all music: these are points which need working on the whole time.

VOCAL TONE

This is where the choirmaster with a good voice scores, because basically the choir works by imitation. Therefore the choirmaster should have his own voice trained (see previous section—choirmaster's asset (page 118)). Nevertheless, some choirmasters produce good tone from their choir even though they have appalling voices themselves: this must be because they have a clear picture of the sound they want, and by trial and error have discovered how to get it out of other people. The first essential of good tone is that one must have a clear perception of the pitch of the note to be sung—in other words, confidence over the notes alone breeds good tone. The second essential is that the voice should come freely through the throat, without being impeded by a stiff jaw or tongue. The third essential is that the singer should breathe properly from the base of the lungs. The fourth essential is that the tone should be generally "forward", with the articulation achieved mainly by the tip of the tongue and the lips—(some consonants like s, z, k are helped by a movement of the jaw). The fifth essential (or resultant) is that the free-sounding voice should pick up resonance in the head, and be able to produce tone loud or soft. How to achieve these things? It is impossible to explain adequately in any book; one needs the live help of a teacher.

The treatment of boys' breaking voices—does one rest the voice for two years or so, or use the boys as altos-cum-librarians?—is also too big a question for this book.

If, nevertheless, a choirmaster *has* to train a choir, and has a poor voice of his own, and is very hazy about good tone, he can (1) make the choir breathe to the base of the lungs; (2) attack consonants d, t, r, l, n by curling up the tip of the tongue and flicking it down; (3) attack consonants m, b, by bringing the lips together and parting them; (4) insist on differentiation between the various vowel sounds; (5) try to achieve a "forward" tone as opposed to a "backward" one. The latter, woolly and ineffectual, artistically very dull, can also produce flat singing. Sharp singing can be due to forcing and inadequate breath support: three obvious solutions are (a) listen more carefully, (b) sing softer, and (c) breathe to the base of the lungs. Sharp singing often occurs on the very first note which, in anxiety (or enthusiasm), has been pushed too high.

TONAL BALANCE

When a choirmaster is conducting, he naturally looks after this: "Tenors too loud, altos not loud enough." When the choirmaster is at the organ, tonal balance is very difficult to achieve. In many churches it is quite difficult to hear the opposite pew clearly owing to the acoustics of the building. If one says "You should always be able to hear your next-door neighbour" this may have an inhibiting effect. Basically, however, everybody should be *aware* of the rest of the choir. There are always "leader types" who are more alert to problems of attack, more sure of the right notes. These members are quite essential to any choir, but they have to be politely kept in check while the less confident members increase their general ability. Sometimes a church choir may have an almost non-existent alto part; one cannot ask everyone to scale down to alto level. (Don't forget that the alto part is a problem which *needs* a solution.)

FOLLOWING A CONDUCTOR

Some singers seem to be able to follow a conductor instinctively; but church choirs are often very bad at this. The reason is that they are more used to working from their ears (and rightly so). To follow a silent beat is an art. Make certain that the choir understands (1) that the actual beat is at the bottom of the gesture — at this point the vowel appears, the consonants having been "got through" before; and (2) that the upbeat gives the tempo — practice is needed at picking this up at different speeds. A difficult anthem like *My soul* (Parry) has constant changes of tempo; each change needs special practice.

FEELING FOR THE PHRASE

Good vowels, good consonants, good rhythm, good tone — but these are only details which are learnt and forgotten, unless they

126

are "locked" in the memory of the choir, as a phrase. Once a phrase has hit the imagination of a singer he never forgets it. For example, in the hymn "Judge eternal, throned in splendour" (tune—*Rhuddlan*) there occurs the phrase "Cleave our darkness with thy sword". After the dotted rhythm "Cleave our dark" has been established, after the vowels EE AH-OO AH etc. have been achieved, after a good KL and a good D have been hit off by the tongue (for "Cleave" and "darkness") etc., there is still this picture of God striking through an area of darkness with a glittering sword. Choirboys may be very hazy about the meaning of "Cleave" (perhaps they have seen a conjuror cut a handkerchief in two in the air?).

The very well-known "Lead me, Lord" (Wesley) promotes a gentle persuasive picture, as of a blind man being guided along by a sighted person. These are the things which add the "extra dimension" to the singing. (But N.B.—do *not* add inspiration until the "mechanical" details are right, otherwise one gets sentimentality,* and it may take years to get rid of it.)

These are only a few of the problems which a choirmaster and his choir may come across. The vexed question of all-male versus mixed-voice choirs must be left to each individual choirmaster to solve. The well-trained choirboy becomes the choirman of the future (so incidentally does the well-trained choirgirl become the contralto or soprano of the future). Some all-male choristers have a horror of ladies with "wobbly voices" in the church choir. But basses and tenors can also have wobbly voices, and a well-trained soprano need not have an uncontrolled *vibrato*. There is nothing like the boy's voice, it is true—but every good voice has its own virtues. Surely what is wanted is quality, and a will to improve where quality is lacking.

* "Sentimentality". The singer tries to express "feeling" with heavy *vibrato*, *portamento*, forced or breathy tone. His desire to be imaginative is excellent, but his methods are wrong.

CHAPTER SEVEN

THE LIBRARY

A church choir library should be like a living organism, constantly shedding unwanted material and acquiring new. One of the first jobs of a choirmaster should be to organise and catalogue his library. If he has never done this before, here are a few words of advice. Do not pack any particular section too tightly, so that there is no room for expansion. When one has come to the end of the A's, leave a space before starting the B's. If there are only horizontal shelves, some form of vertical partitioning is essential, such as hardboard fitted into grooves, or wooden partitions nailed from above and below. Give the pigeon-holes numbers or letters, and make a complete catalogue or card index. "Hear my prayer"–Arcadelt–Locker No. 1. Settings of the canticles, R.S.C.M. volumes, etc., could perhaps be kept separate, but they should appear on the card index, so that anyone can find them. Each set of music is best kept in a folder or envelope; good folders or envelopes will in the long run save money. A library looks better with a little colour; different coloured folders also make it easy to find a work quickly ("Jesu, joy of Man's desiring" is in a *red* folder). Even better — the R.S.C.M. supplies cardboard box files; these are, of course, a little more expensive.

Each new choirmaster has different views on what is worth singing and what isn't. All the music which is unlikely to be sung should be taken out, stacked elsewhere, and carefully catalogued; the regular repertoire will then have space to breathe. Be very careful about throwing music away while there is still room to store it; the next choirmaster may have completely different views on what is good or bad.

A choirmaster should be given an allowance to buy new anthems and replace worn out music. Honorary Treasurers of the Parish, please allow the choirmaster a little room to experiment!

One of the choir should be appointed Librarian, and this job must have a certain flavour of distinction about it. A badge? Name on the choir notice-board? Each new work as it is added needs to be catalogued by the Librarian and stamped "Pewbury Parish Library", and the choir must be lectured severely that it is wrong, nay a mortal sin, to build up a store of music belonging to the church on one's own shelves at home.

PERIODS THAT MUST BE REPRESENTED ON THE SHELVES

BEFORE PALESTRINA

Composers like G. de Machaut (1300–1377), Dunstable (1390–1453), Dufay (1400–1474), Ockeghem (1430–1495), J. des Prés (1445–1521), Fayrfax (1464–1521), L. Power (fifteenth century), Taverner (1495–1545).

PALESTRINA AND THE POLYPHONIC SCHOOL

Possibly the four great names are Palestrina, Vittoria, Lassus and Byrd. But there are so many others—Gabrieli (both uncle and nephew), Sweelinck, Hassler, Schütz (the last two, both pupils of Gabrieli), and Monteverdi (bridging the gap between this period and the next); Jacob Handl, Vecchi, and the enormous Tudor school in England—Morley, Tallis, Tomkins, Weelkes, to mention only a few. This is the great period of *unaccompanied* vocal music.

BACH AND HANDEL

Apart from little pieces like "Jesu, joy" and "Flocks in pastures", there should be at least two of the two hundred or so extant Bach Church cantatas, etc., on the shelves. *Messiah* should of course be there, and some separate choruses by Handel.

After representing something by Purcell and Monteverdi, there are the lesser English composers, e.g. Blow, Croft, Greene, Humfrey. The list on pages 146–147 has some suggestions for German cantatas of this period (and slightly earlier), especially by composers like Buxtehude, which are admirable and fairly easy.

THE ROMANTIC ERA

This is full of great composers—Schumann, Brahms, Berlioz, Dvořák, Wagner—but few of these composers wrote much music which is simple enough for the average church choir. Elgar,

Mendelssohn and Tchaikovsky are "big" names, who have produced some simpler music. There are scores of English composers who belong more to a "Victorian" era than to a Romantic one; much of this music, which occupies a good deal of space at present (1967) on the shelves of the average church choir, should be thinned out—gradually—to make way for other music. Much of the music of such composers as Bairstow, Barnby, Dunhill, Dykes, Elvey, Garrett, Gaul, Goss, Lloyd, Macfarren, Mackenzie, Monk, Oakeley, Ouseley, Smart, Stainer, Tours, Turle, and Walmisley has served its purpose, and worked hard and well; it was carefully written and relatively simple—all it lacked was the essential inspiration which the greater music has.

EDWARDIAN

Towards the end of the century, and stretching into the present twentieth century, a group of composers were trying hard to rescue English music from its rather low state. These included Walford Davies, Charles Wood, Parry, Stanford, Vaughan Williams, Holst, John Ireland, and later Herbert Howells, Bliss, Finzi and Rubbra. Similar efforts were also being made in other countries; the list could be protracted endlessly. Not only was research proceeding forwards; it was also going further back towards medieval music and plainsong.

THE TWENTIETH CENTURY

This is very interested in choral music; much of this is too advanced for church congregation and choir. There are, of course, composers living today who write in Edwardian style. Modern composers, however, who are already to some extent acceptable include Britten, Walton, Kodály and Tippett.

It would be possible, at this point, to append a huge list of music labelled (1) Easy; (2) Fairly Easy; (3) Fairly Difficult; (4) Difficult; (5) Very Difficult. This grading, though very useful, is obviously relative to the choir. One of the contentions of the writers of this book is that music performed in the church should be primarily good music. By good, we mean music that inspires, charms, delights, intrigues—in fact, music that challenges or persuades the congregation to listen. If the music is also simple, so much the better; but it is a mistake (in our opinion) to choose music simply because it is easy to perform. The second question is "quality" of performance. It is part of the process of learning: "If only we had remembered to plan our start and practise it— does the organist give the first chord or the first four bars?" . . . Next time (we hope) a lesson will have been learnt for the future. This requires patience on everybody's part: like a mother watching her child learn to walk and talk—so is a choir learning to *perform*. The "mother" is the priest and congregation, the child is the choir. During this learning period, the priest and congregation can be sympathetic and encouraging, comparing each performance with the previous performance—"the words were so much better, the rhythm, the attack—the last chord was beautifully in tune", etc.—looking always for positive improvements. As soon as this learning period is over (and every choirmaster may have a patch of this), anthems now become graded. Grade 1 = Fairly Difficult; Grade 2 = Very Difficult; Grade 3 = Impossible. Gradually these levels change. While this standard is relatively low, there is not much music available. We contend that easy music without quality may be useful to practise and learn, but not to perform. Our first list therefore consists of good, easy music.

GOOD, EASY MUSIC

CAROLS

As pointed out in *The Oxford Book of Carols*, carols are available for most Festivals of the year, not just for Christmas. There is a list of carol books towards the end of this chapter.

GOOD HYMNS

An excellent way of introducing a new hymn tune is to sing it first as an anthem; but there are some good hymns which, if variety is introduced in the arrangement, are almost better as easy anthems.

Here are some suggested arrangements for carols and hymns, assuming that four verses have been selected.

(1) Accompanied by organ: (*a*) SATB; (*b*) S + A unis. (melody); (*c*) T + B unis. (melody); (*d*) SATB.

(2) (*a*) Full unison, accompanied; (*b*) SATB, unaccompanied; (*c*) S. soloist first two lines—T. soloist last two lines, accompanied; (*d*) SATB, accompanied.

(3) Accompanied by organ: (*a*) S. soloist, ATB humming; (*b*) SATB; (*c*) T. soloist (melody); (*d*) unison.

(4) Hymn with refrain (e.g. *Hilariter*): (*a*) SATB; (*b*) lines one and three, S + A (unison), (or S. soloist). Refrain full (unison); (*c*) Lines one and three, T + B (unison), (or T. soloist). Refrain full (unison); (*d*) SATB.

(5) Hymn with refrain: (*a*) SATB; (*b*) Lines one and three, T. soloist, SAB hum lines one and three, but break into words for lines two and four; (*c*) S. soloist (same pattern as verse 2); (*d*) SATB lines one and three—unison lines two and four.

The possible schemes are endless: the available "methods" with which one juggles are (*a*) full SATB; (*b*) full unison; (*c*) upper voices only, unison; (*d*) lower voices only, unison; (*e*) a soloist unaccompanied; (*f*) a soloist accompanied by organ; (*g*) a soloist accompanied by the three other parts humming; (*h*) variations. To these can be added *p*, *mf*, and *f*.

A FEW EASY ANTHEMS

This list, and the lists of less easy anthems which follow, contain only a few suggestions. It is hoped that the reader will add his own selections to the lists, which are not exhaustive. The anthems are arranged according to period.

ANTHEMS

Grade One—Easy

EARLY

ARCADELT

Give ear unto my prayer (*Ave Maria*), (Nov.).

R. STONES

The Lord's Prayer (Nov.).

POLYPHONIC

FARRANT

Hide not Thou Thy face (O.U.P.).
Call to remembrance (O.U.P.).

HILTON

Lord, for Thy tender mercy's sake (O.U.P.).

TALLIS

If Ye love me (O.U.P.).

TYE

O come, ye servants of the Lord (Nov.).
Cibavit Illos (Cary).

BAROQUE

BACH

Jesu, joy of man's desiring (O.U.P.).
Awake us, Lord, and hasten (O.U.P.).
Zion hears her watchmen's voices (Nov.).
(These are extended chorales—choir easy, organ not so easy.)
If Thou art near (Bist du bei mir), arr. W. H. Harris (Nov.).

BLOW

O pray for the peace of Jerusalem—S solo and chorus (Nov.).

M. GREENE

Thou visitest the earth—Harvest (Nov.).

LOTTI

Regina coeli (Cary).

CLASSICAL

ATTWOOD

Come, Holy Ghost (Nov.).
Turn Thy face from my sins (Nov.).

MOZART

Jesu, Word of God Incarnate (Ave verum) (Nov.).

ROMANTIC — VICTORIAN

OUSELEY

Jerusalem on high (Hagar) (Nov.).
From the rising of the sun (Nov.).

133

S. S. WESLEY

Lead me, Lord (from Praise the Lord, O my soul) (Nov.).

BUCK

O Lord God — S solo, and SSA — Sexagesima (Nov.).

G. JACOBS

Brother James's air — arrt. (O.U.P.).

LEY

The Lord ascendeth — arrt. Schicht (Nov.).
The strife is o'er — arrt. Vulpius (O.U.P.).

VAUGHAN WILLIAMS

O taste and see (O.U.P.).

Grade Two — Fairly Easy

EARLY

J. E. D'ESTERRE PAUL

Magnificat and Nunc Dimittis with Faux-Bourdons (Nov.).

MUNDAY

O Lord, the Maker of all thing (Nov. and O.U.P.).

TALLIS

O Lord, give Thy Holy Spirit (O.U.P.).
(Also plainsong settings of the Canticles and Communion
Service — *R.S.C.M. Recommended List.*)

POLYPHONIC

ASOLA

Ave Rex Noster — TTB (Ches.).

DOWLAND

Jesu Lord! Who through my infant days (Nov.).

FESTA

Sancta Maria—SSA (Ches.).

J. HANDL

The righteous perisheth—All Saints' Day (Bos.).

HASSLER

Dixit Maria (Ches.).

PALESTRINA

O Saviour of the World (Nov.).
Alma Redemptoris Mater (Ches.).
Adoramus te Christi—TTBB (Ches.).

VIADANA

O Sacrum Convivium—TTBB (Ches.).

WEELKES

Let Thy merciful ears (O.U.P.).

BAROQUE

BACH

King of Glory, King of Peace, arr. Harris (O.U.P.).

BLOW

Let my prayer come up (S. & B.).

HANDEL

O lovely peace—SS (Nov.).
Lord of our being—S or SS or SATB (Nov.).

PURCELL

Thou knowest, Lord (Nov.).
Rejoice in the Lord (Nov.). (Easy for the choir, solos more difficult.)
Evening Hymn—Unis. or SATB (O.U.P.).

WISE

Prepare ye the way (O.U.P.).

BEETHOVEN

Creation's Hymn (Nov.).

BOYCE

O turn away mine eyes (O.U.P.).

ROMANTIC — VICTORIAN

MENDELSSOHN

He that shall endure (*Elijah*) (Nov.).
If with all your hearts (Nov.).

FRANCK

Panis Angelicus — two-part (Ashdown).

MODERN

STRAVINSKY

Ave Maria (B. & H.).
Pater Noster (B. & H.).

Grade Three — Fairly Difficult

EARLY

BLITHEMAN

In Peace — Motet for Compline (Nov.).

MEDIEVAL CAROLS

Anon., ed. J. Stevens. In sets of two–three, from Volume IV of
Musica Britannica (S. & B.).

L. POWER

Ave Regina Coelorum — SAT (S. & B.).

REDFORD

Rejoice in the Lord — SATB — Advent (Nov.).

AICHINGER

Factus est Repente — Whitsun or general (Cary).

AMNER

The heav'ns stood all amazed — SSATB (S. & B.).

ANERIO

Jesus, once for our salvation (Nov.).

BYRD

Ave, Verum Corpus (S. & B.).

CONSTANTINI

Confitemini Domino — TTB (A. Bank-Ches.).

GIBBONS

Almighty and everlasting God (O.U.P.).
O Lord, increase my faith (Nov.).

GOUDIMEL

Psalm 105: O magnify and honour the Lord (Bos.).

J. HANDL

Behold thou shalt conceive — Christmas (Bos.).

HASSLER

Cantate Domino — TTBB (Ches.).

MONTEVERDI

Angelus ad pastores ait — SAT or SAA (Bos.).

SWEELINCK

Gaudete Omnes — SSATB (Bos.).
Laudate Dominum — SSATB (Bos.).
Psalm 105 (Bos.).

TALLIS

Gloria Patri (Nov.).

WEELKES

David's Lamentation (Bos.).

BACH

Flocks in green pastures abiding (O.U.P.).
Psalm 121, No. 1 (Cantata 37), No. 2 (Cantata 71) (Pat.).
What God ordains is best of all (Nov.).
    (Slightly harder extended chorales.)
Praise Him — Harvest (Pat.).

HAYDN

The Heavens are telling (Nov.).
God of Light (*The Seasons*) (Nov.).

GREENE

Lord, let me know mine end — Funeral (Nov. and O.U.P.).

Unison

BACH

Saviour Shepherd (O.U.P.).

HANDEL

I know that my Redeemer liveth (*Messiah*) (Nov.).

CLASSICAL

ARNE

Here sons of Jacob (*Judith*) — SSATB (O.U.P.).

CROFT

God is gone up with a merry noise — Verse, SSAATB (Nov.).

SCHUBERT

The Lord is my Shepherd — SS, SSAA or SATB (Nov.).

BALAKIREFF

O send forth Thy light — Lent (Bay. & Fer.).

BENNETT

God is a Spirit (Nov.).

BERLIOZ

Thou must leave Thy lowly dwelling (Nov.).

GOSS

O Saviour of the world (Nov.).
If we believe that Jesus died (Nov.).
Almighty and merciful God (Nov.).
God so loved the world (Nov.).

MACPHERSON

Shepherd's Cradle Song (Cur.).

STANFORD

Canticles in B Flat (Nov.).

PARRATT

Give rest, O Christ (*Contakion*) — TTBB (Nov.).

TCHAIKOVSKY

Holy, Holy, Holy! Lord God Almighty (*Hymn to the Trinity*, No. 1) (Nov.).
The Crown of Roses (*The Oxford Book of Carols*) (O.U.P.).

WALMISLEY

Magnificat and Nunc Dimittis in D Minor (Nov.).

S. S. WESLEY

Cast me not away from Thy presence — SSATTB — Lent or general use (Nov.).
O Lord, my God (*Solomon's Prayer*) (Nov.).
Blessed be the God and Father — SSATB (Nov.).
Wash me throughly (Nov.).

MARTIN SHAW

O Christ, Who holds the open gate — Harvest (Nov.).

VAUGHAN WILLIAMS

Lullaby from *Hodie* — SSA (O.U.P.).

Grade Four — Difficult

EARLY

TALLIS

Into Thine hand, O Lord (S. & B.).

POLYPHONIC

BATTEN

Hear my prayer, O God (O.U.P.).

BYRD

O Magnum Mysterium (S. & B., Ches.).

GIBBONS

O clap your hands (O.U.P.).
This is the record of John — A or T solo and SSATB (Nov.).

PALESTRINA

Exaltabo Te, Domine (Latin only) — SSATB (Nov.).

PHILIPS

The Lord ascendeth (O.U.P.).

SHEPHERD

Haec Dies — SATTBar.B (Ches.).

SWEELINCK

Hodie Christus Natus Est (Born Today) — five voices (Nov.).

WEELKES

Alleluia, I heard a voice (O.U.P.).

R. WHYTE

O Praise God in His holiness (O.U.P.).

BAROQUE

BACH

Crucifixus (B Minor Mass) (Nov.).

PURCELL

O God, Thou art my God (Nov.).
Save me, O God, for Thy name's sake — SSATTB (Nov.).

CLASSICAL

BATTISHILL

O Lord, look down from Heaven — five voices (Nov.).

BOYCE

O Where Shall Wisdom — Verse, SSATB (Nov.).

HANDEL

How excellent the name (*Saul*) (Nov.).
Let their celestial concerts (*Samson*) (Nov.).
Then round about the starry throne (*Samson*) (Pat.).

ROMANTIC — VICTORIAN

BRAHMS

Ave Maria — SSAA (Bos.).
How lovely are Thy dwellings (Requiem) (Nov.).

S. S. WESLEY

Cast me not away from Thy presence — SSATTB (Nov.).

EDWARDIAN

HOLST

Ave Maria — SSSSAAAA (Bos.).

MARTIN SHAW

O Glorious Maid (Cur.).

PARRY

I was glad when they said unto me (Coronation Anthem) (Nov.).

STANFORD

Justorum Animae (B. & H.).
Glorious and Powerful—Motet (S. & B.).
Beati Quorum Via—SSATBB (B. & H.).

MODERN

BRITTEN

A hymn to the Virgin—double SATB (B. & H.).

S. CAMPBELL

Sing we merrily (Nov.).

Grade Five—Very Difficult

EARLY

DUNSTABLE

Sancta Maria—TTB (S. & B.).

L. POWER

Beata Progenies—ATB (S. & B.).

TALLIS

In Jejunio et Fletu (Ches.).
Salvator Mundi (Ches.).

TAVERNER

Dum Transisset Sabbatum (S. & B.).

POLYPHONIC

BYRD

This is the day (ed. Terry)—SSATTB (Nov.).
Sing joyfully unto God (ed. Bennett)—SSATTB (Nov.).

RICHARD DERING

O all that pass by—SSATTB (Bos.).
Say, O shepherds, whom saw ye? (ed. Terry)—SSATTB (Nov.).

GIBBONS

Hosanna to the Son of David (O.U.P.).

HASSLER

Rejoice ye heavens—TTBB (Nov.).

LASSUS

Salve, Regina—six-part (Ches.).

PALESTRINA

Dum Complerentur (Latin and English—ed. A. G. Petti)
(Ches.).

PHILLIPS

While organs made harmony (ed. Terry)—SSATB (Nov.).

TOMKINS

O sing unto the Lord a new song—SSAATBB (Sch.).

VECCHI

Alleluya, Sing Praises—SATTB (Bos.).

WEELKES

Hosanna to the Son of David—SSATBB (O.U.P.).
When David heard—Motet for SSAATB unacc. (Nov.).

BAROQUE

BACH

O Praise the Lord, all ye nations (Psalm 117, Motet No. 6)
(Nov.).

ROMANTIC — VICTORIAN

BRAHMS

O Rend the heavens and help us, Lord (Nov.).

143

VAUGHAN WILLIAMS

Valiant for truth (O.U.P.).
Prayer to the Father of Heaven (O.U.P.).

MODERN

BRITTEN

Jubilate Deo in C (O.U.P.).
Te Deum in C (O.U.P.).
Missa Brevis in D—SSA (B. & H.).

FRICKER

Two carols: Mary is a Lady Bright; In Excelsis Gloria (O.U.P.).

HOPKINS

Carillon—SSAATTBB (Ches.).

HOWELLS

Collegium Regale (setting of the Te Deum and Jubilate) (Nov.).

JOUBERT

O Lorde, the Maker of al thing (Nov.).

KODALY

Jesus and the Traders (U.M.P.).
All men drew near—Christmas carol (O.U.P.).

MAXWELL DAVIES

Movements from *O Magnum Mysterium* (Sch.).

OLDHAM

A Festival Anthem—S or T solo, SSATB (B. & H.).

SCHOENBERG

Dreimal Tausend Jahre (Thrice in a Thousand Years) (German and English) (Sch.).

SEIBER

Missa Brevis (Cur.).

Magnificat and Nunc Dimittis (*Collegium Sancti Johannis Canta-brigiense*) (Sch.).

These lists are necessarily very incomplete.

HOW TO GET HOLD OF THE WORKS OF EARLY COMPOSERS

(1) Ask in one's Public Library for books on Dufay, Josquin des Pres, Guillaume de Machaut, etc. (2) Some North American publishers have printed these works: e.g. "The Desoff Choir Series" (Mercury Music Corporation) which may be obtained through Schott & Co. (3) *The History of Music in Sound* (H.M.V.) is a series of records covering the whole of music. Each period has a complementary handbook with musical examples (O.U.P.) which may be purchased with or without the records. (4) *The New Oxford History of Music* (O.U.P.), of which the first three volumes (covering a period of up to 1540) have been published (up to 1966), contains many examples. (5) The British Museum. (6) *Historical Anthology of Music*, by Willi Apel and A. T. Davison (Harvard–O.U.P.).

LARGER SACRED WORKS

It is only natural for church choirs to wish to perform the great sacred works on special occasions, and for this it may be necessary to combine with other choirs. This arrangement is admirable, as it means that (apart from there being more singers) there are at least two organists available for all important jobs of accompanying, conducting and organising. Sections of these large works may of course be very useful for anthems.

The following is a suggested list. A larger list may be obtained by extracting the sacred works from the list of works to be performed by societies belonging to the National Federation of Music Societies (see page 169). The list that follows has also been organised into periods.

MEDIEVAL PLAYS (WITH MUSIC)

Herod, ed. W. L. Smoldon (S. & B.).

The Play of Herod, ed. Noah Greenberg and W. L. Smoldon (O.U.P.).

Visitatio Sepulchri, ed. and tr. W. L. Smoldon (O.U.P.).

The Play of Daniel, ed. Noah Greenberg (O.U.P.).

Early settings of the Passion Story: e.g. Passion according to St. Matthew (Richard Davey) from *The Eton Choirbook* (S. & B.).

The story is sung in plainsong by a soloist, the choral interludes being confined to those portions of the narrative where the crowd or the priests, etc., speak. There is also no reason why the narrative should not be *spoken* in English, and the choral portions retained.

TAVERNER

Mass: *The Western Wind,* ed. Philip Brett (S. & B.).

POLYPHONIC

BYRD

Masses for Three, Four and Five Voices (S. & B.).

The Great Service (O.U.P.).

Passion according to St. John, ed. E. H. Fellowes and Thurston Dart (S. & B.). See remarks on Davey's Passion, above.

A. GABRIELI

Missa Brevis (Ches.).

SCHÜTZ

The St. Matthew Passion (in English), ed. Imogen Holst and Peter Pears (O.U.P.).

The St. Luke Passion (in English), ed. Paul Steinitz and John Battley (O.U.P.).

The Passion according to St. John, ed. Imogen Holst and Peter Pears (O.U.P.).

The Seven Last Words From The Cross, ed. N. McCabe and Paul Steinitz (O.U.P.).

Symphonia Sacra: Mein Sohn Warum Hast Du Uns das Getan (German and English), ed. Paul Steinitz (O.U.P.).

PALESTRINA

Missa Papae Marcelli (English and Latin) (Nov.).
Missa Aeterna Christi Munera (English) (Nov.).
Missa Brevis (Latin) (Ches.).
Stabat Mater (Latin) (Nov.).

BAROQUE

BACH

St. John Passion (Nov.).
St. Matthew Passion (Nov.).
Mass in B Minor (Nov.).
Christmas Oratorio—six sections (Nov.).
Magnificat (Nov.).
"Jesu, Priceless Treasure" (Nov.).

Cantatas, especially:
"Praise Our God, Who Reigns in Heaven" (No. 11) (Nov.).
"My Spirit Was in Heaviness" (No. 21) (Nov.).
– "Sleepers, Wake!" (No. 140) (Nov.).
"God's Time is the Best" (No. 106) (Nov.).

BUXTEHUDE

Das Neugeborene Kindelein (Nov.).

HANDEL

– *Messiah* (Nov.).
– *Judas* (Nov.).
Samson (Nov.).
Saul (Nov.).
Chandos Anthems (Nov.) etc., etc.

PERGOLESI

Stabat Mater (Latin and English) (Nov., or O.U.P.).

PURCELL

Te Deum (Nov.).

D. SCARLATTI

Stabat Mater (Latin) (Peters).

VIVALDI

Gloria (Latin and English) (Chap.).

CLASSICAL

HAYDN

The Creation (Nov.).
Passion (*Seven Last Words*) (Nov.).
- Mass No. 3 in D (*Nelson* or *Imperial*) (Nov.).
Mass No. 2 in C (*Paukenmesse* or *Kettledrum*) (*Missa in Tempora Belli*) (Nov.).

MOZART

Mass in D Minor (Requiem) (Nov.).
Mass in C (No. 1) (Nov.).
Mass in G (No. 12) (Nov.).
- *Vesperae Solemnes de Confessore* (Breit.).

ROMANTIC — VICTORIAN

BERLIOZ

The Childhood of Christ (Nov.).

BRAHMS

- Requiem (English) (Nov. or Hin.).
Song of Destiny (Nov.).

BRUCKNER

Mass in E Minor (Latin) (Peters).

DVORAK

Stabat Mater (English) (Nov.).

ELGAR

The Dream of Gerontius (Nov.).
"Great is the Lord" (Psalm 48) (Nov.).

148

MENDELSSOHN

Elijah (Nov.).
St. Paul (Nov.).
Hear My Prayer (Nov.).
- *Hymn of Praise* (Nov.).

ROSSINI

Petite Messe Solemnelle (Latin) (Ric.).
Stabat Mater (Latin or English) (Nov.).

VERDI

Requiem (Latin) (Ric.).
Quattro Pezzi Sacri (Latin) (Ric.).

EDWARDIAN

FINZI

In Terra Pax (B. & H.).
Magnificat (B. & H.).

HOWELLS

Hymnus Paradisi (Nov.).

HOLST

Christmas Day (Nov.).

OLDROYD

Stabat Mater (Latin and English) (O.U.P.).

RUBBRA

Missa in Honorem Sancti Dominici (Latin) (Leng.).

VAUGHAN WILLIAMS

Benedicite (O.U.P.).
Fantasia on Christmas Carols (S. & B.).
This Day (*Hodie*) (O.U.P.).
The Old Hundredth psalm tune (O.U.P.).
Mass in G Minor (Cur.).

JEAN BERGER

Brazilian Psalm (Chap.).

BRITTEN

- *A Ceremony of Carols* — SSA or SATB (B. & H.).
A Boy was Born (O.U.P.).
Rejoice in the Lamb (B. & H.).
St. Nicholas (B. & H.).
War Requiem (B. & H.).
A Wedding Anthem (B. & H.).

BLISS

The Beatitudes (Nov.).

CAAMANO

Psalmus 114 (B. & H.).

COPLAND

In the Beginning — MS solo, unacc. choir (B. & H.).

HOLST

The Hymn of Jesus (S. & B.).

HONEGGER

King David (Ches.).
Joan of Arc at the Stake (U.M.P.).

JOUBERT

Three Motets (*Pro Pace*) (Latin) (Nov.).

KODALY

Te Deum (Univ.).
Psalmus Hungaricus (Univ.).
Pange Lingua (Univ.).

PETRASSI

Magnificat (Ric.).

STRAVINSKY

- *Symphony of Psalms* (B. & H.).
  Mass (B. & H.).

TIPPETT

A Child of Our Time (Sch.).

WALTON

Coronation Te Deum (Latin) (O.U.P.).
Gloria (Latin) (O.U.P.).
Belshazzar's Feast (O.U.P.).

MODERN MUSICAL DRAMA

MENOTTI

Amahl and the Night Visitors (Schirmer–Chap.). Christmas opera
in one act.

LA MONTAINE

Novellis Novellis (Schirmer–Chap.). Pageant opera.

BRITTEN

Noye's Fludde (B. & H.).

ROMAN CATHOLIC CHURCH MUSIC FROM THE NETHERLANDS

Convent choirs, or small Catholic choirs with upper voices only,
may be looking for fresh music, which is known to publishers as
"for two or three equal voices". Some very interesting music of
this kind is at present being produced in Holland, by composers
such as Andriessen, Overbeek, Schmit, Strategier, etc.

This music, which is not too difficult, may be obtained through
the English agents, Hinrichsen. We would recommend:

Andriessen, *Missa in hon. Ss. Cordis* (two equal voices), *Laudes
Vespertinae* (seasonal motets for two–three equal voices).

Overbeek, *Veneremur* (five motets for three equal voices), *Missa
Maria Gloriosa* (two equal voices).

P. Schmit, *Missa kinder Swyght* (two–three equal voices).

H. Strategier, *Missa Caritas benigna est* (two equal voices).

(All the above are published by Wed. J. R. van Rossum,
Utrecht, Holland.)

As a change from an anthem (sung), if there are good instrumentalists available, it is sometimes very delightful to have a string quartet, or violin and piano, flute and piano, etc. It is quite impossible to list all the available music, some of which could be in the library.

CAROL BOOKS

The Oxford Book of Carols (O.U.P.). One hundred and ninety-seven carols for Christmas, Easter, Nativity, etc.

Carols for Choirs (O.U.P.). Fifty Christmas carols, mostly for mixed voices; the text of the Nine Lessons is printed as an appendix.

The Oxford Book of Carols for Schools (O.U.P.). Fifty carols selected from the complete book and arranged for unison singing; also published for various combinations of recorders.

The Oxford S.A.B. Carol Book (O.U.P.). Forty well-known carols arranged by Reginald Jacques, mainly from *The Oxford Book of Carols*.

The Cambridge Carol Book (S.P.C.K.).

Descant Carol Books, Nos. 1, 2 & 3 (Nov.).

Carols by R. R. Terry (Cur.).

The R.S.C.M. Carol Book (R.S.C.M.). Ten carols, with suggestions for a Nine Lessons carol service.

The Saint Nicholas Carol Book (R.S.C.M.). Twelve carols, with suggestions for a Nine Lessons carol service.

University Carol Book (Freeman).* Over two hundred carols, edited by Dr. Erik Routley; they are arranged according to the Church season, and the inclusion of a few hymns makes provision for services of lessons and carols.

The English Carol Book (Mowbray). Fifty-four carols for mixed voices, edited by Martin Shaw and Percy Dearmer.

The Cowley Carol Book (Mowbray). One hundred and two carols for Christmas, Easter and Ascension-tide, compiled and arranged by G. R. Woodward and Charles Wood.

Traditional Carols, arr. Imogen Holst (4 sets: O.U.P.). Twenty-four carols arranged for three- and four-part women's voices.

* Messrs. Freeman also publish several collections of carols arranged for the recorder.

Carols of Today (O.U.P.). Seventeen original carols for mixed voices, set by British composers.

Sing Nowell (Nov.). Further modern carols.

A series of Christmas carol orchestrations (six popular carols arranged for full orchestra or smaller combinations by Victor Fleming) is published by Galliard.

ANTHEM BOOKS

Several collections of anthems are published; these may sometimes be found useful, especially in smaller churches of all denominations where the cost of buying separate anthems may be too great.

The Church Anthem Book (O.U.P.). One hundred anthems, ed. by Walford Davies and Henry G. Ley.

A Sixteenth-Century Anthem Book (O.U.P.). Twenty anthems for four voices.

The Oxford Easy Anthem Book (O.U.P.). Fifty anthems, easy or of only moderate difficulty.

Anthems for men's voices (2 vols., O.U.P.). Forty-seven anthems chosen from the fifteenth to eighteenth centuries.

The Novello Anthem Book (Nov.). Fifty anthems, available in staff notation or tonic solfa.

Short and Easy Anthems (Nov.). Fifteen anthems.

Congregational Anthem Book, ed. Eric Thiman (Independent Press).

The "Aldersgate" Anthem Books (Epworth Press). No. 3: 17 Anthems from the "Choir Series"; No. 4: 12 Anthems from the "Choir Series".

With such a long list of music to be performed (and this is only a fragment of the enormous sacred repertoire), composers may feel that there is no need for additions. Nothing could be further from the truth. (1) Good music in a contemporary idiom is always needed—music making fresh use of rhythm, harmony, melody, texture, dynamics, etc. (2) There is a special call for simple twentieth-century music (as opposed to some music written today in a nineteenth-century or Edwardian style). (3) What about small cantatas with simple instrumental accompaniment (please, a fresh choice of instruments)? These cantatas (these are only suggestions) could avoid *solos*—but make plenty of use of vocal trios, quartets, etc., playing these smaller groups off against the full choir, in the manner of a verse anthem. Little instrumental interludes (*ritornelli*) on recorders played by children of the choir (and adults)? Trumpets and other brass instruments sound magnificent in a church. Simple material, used with imagination.

CHAPTER EIGHT

HUMAN RELATIONSHIPS AND
OFFICIAL BODIES

"By this all men shall know you are my disciples—if you have love one to another." Organist, flower-arranger, minister, church cleaner, bellringer, member of congregation, hon. treasurer, magazine editor, choirman, scoutmaster, Sunday School teacher, etc. However, human relationships within a church are often no better than in other human organisations.

There are several difficulties. First, some "official" members are paid (ministers, organists, etc.); others (sidesmen, readers, etc.) are not. In some churches, choirs are paid; in others a few members are paid and the others not; in the majority, none are paid. Voluntary workers may feel superior (or inferior) to paid workers. "The body is not one member, but many. The eye cannot say to the hand, I have no need of thee . . ." But the practice of paying some members and not others is fraught with potential difficulties.

Another problem: who is in charge? Basically, of course, the incumbent (vicar, priest or minister), and the appointment of the organist is legally in his hands. As long as the man-in-charge is a strong character, strong in Christ, all goes well. But a weak, indeterminate man-in-charge can be as bad within a church as within any other organisation, especially if petty-minded officials strive for their quota of "power" or "influence". Perhaps it may help to suggest some limitations of "power" as these affect Church music—the subject of this book.

The pamphlet *Organists in Parish Churches* (Church Information Board), which is issued by the Authority of the Diocesan Bishops of the Provinces of Canterbury and York, makes it clear that, in the Church of England, the selection of hymns, etc. is to be controlled by the incumbent; the tunes may be chosen by the organist, and approved by the incumbent (see also "The Legal Position of the Organist" in *English Church Music*, R.S.C.M.,

1964). Nevertheless, owing to his innumerable duties, it is not unknown for the incumbent to delegate some of these responsibilities. As far as the Authorities within his particular church are concerned, he will probably insist that:

(1) The organist is the expert in musical affairs. In so far as the general conduct of the music is concerned, he is the man-in-charge. It is quite common for the incumbent, in fact, to delegate the choosing of hymns and tunes to the organist. But whenever the incumbent wishes to have some special hymn, psalm or anthem, the organist is "under orders", and must do his best to provide the music—but he must have adequate time to rehearse unfamiliar music. In other words, if the music is difficult the organist needs several weeks' warning; if it is relatively easy, he should have time to look at the music before he appears at the practice. It is not fair to hand an organist music on the Friday before the Sunday on which it is to be sung.

Exceptionally, the incumbent may be more expert at music than the organist. In this difficult situation we would suggest that the incumbent should keep the choosing of the hymns, psalms (even anthems if need be) entirely in his own hands—giving the organist adequate time to prepare the music (ideally planning out all music a month in advance), or that the incumbent should appoint another organist who is musically superior to himself.

(2) If the organist is inadequate in any way, the only man who may tell him this is the incumbent. The following are cases in point: (*a*) The organist's voluntaries are inadequate; (*b*) the organist turns up late for service; (*c*) the choir behaves badly during the service; (*d*) the choir is singing out of tune; (*e*) the various members of the choir do not listen to each other and do not keep together; (*f*) the congregation cannot sing the hymns (the pitch is too high, or the unfamiliar tunes are too numerous); (*g*) the organist is consistently rude to other church officials; (*h*) the organ is too loud; or too soft. It is only fair to remember that an organist, when at the organ, may find it difficult to judge whether the organ is loud or soft enough; and this is partly a question of taste anyway.

Ideally, these problems should be solved by a regular meeting between the organist and the incumbent, when all problems can be discussed. An organist can become very depressed by too much criticism, especially from people who "know what they like, but have never played an instrument or sung", and it is one of the duties of the incumbent to protect him from this. If an organist receives a complaint, he should ask the person to pass it on to the incumbent, so that they may then discuss it together. This automatically cuts down trivial criticism (not, alas, all of it).

Minister and organist work better together if the minister (or one of the clergy) can attend the choir practices regularly. This greatly encourages organist and choir, and also helps a "united front".

(3) *Hymn Boards, Hymn (Service) Sheets, etc.* The organist is responsible, but should delegate these jobs to head choirboys, choirmen, servers, etc. Preparing service sheets, changing hymn boards, distributing hymn sheets, etc., often occurs at a time when an organist should be playing a voluntary. Inefficient delegation leads to an organist trying to do three jobs at once. The minister should help a harassed organist—not all musicians possess the gift of delegation to an adequate degree.

(4) *Visiting Clergy and Deputy Organists.* These always want to know whether there are amens after the hymns; how often the phrase "The Lord be with you" occurs during the Communion Service; is the creed sung or spoken; is there an opening hymn; is the second Lord's Prayer omitted; etc., etc. These minor details, which differ from church to church (and there are similar variations in the Free Church services) need tabulating clearly on a list, so that a visiting minister or organist can immediately be clear on these small points.

(5) A meeting should be held to lay down various routines which apply in ceremonial of any sort. It requires co-operation between all the church officials: especially in processions. Rehearsals are necessary until the routine is established and confident. People get very worried in processions if they do not know where they are going and what they have to do. Organists/ministers are usually so run off their feet during the week that they do not always anticipate the difficulties which may arise on the following Sunday, and ministers/organists easily get irritated if all their careful rehearsal is suddenly swept aside by their opposite number.

(6) Should servers, etc., sing? By all means, if they fit in with the choir, but the organist is entitled to complain if a server sings consistently out of tune.

157

(7) If a large musical scheme is afoot—e.g. Bach's St. John Passion on Good Friday—on which a large amount of money is being spent (orchestra and soloists) then, provided relationships are good within the church, a lively committee can be formed to deal with finance, sale of tickets, printing of programmes, etc. Should a congregation be forced to buy tickets to attend a performance of a large religious work? Entrance to a church should be free, but members can be encouraged to help with the financial side of a large undertaking. A frank statement at the end of a performance, and a collection, can often redress the balance. (It should be noted that the New and Revised Canons of the Church of England stipulate, inter alia, that before a concert, etc., shall be held in any church or chapel, the minister must consult the local authorities concerned with the precautions against fire, etc., and obtain their consent.)

SALARY

An organist's salary is generally considered quite out of proportion to the number of hours he dedicates to his work. However, when a sum has been agreed upon, the organist should be quite clear in his mind about extra services. He should either give his help freely and willingly, or else stipulate that he will require extra remuneration for the extra services which will inevitably occur from time to time.

HOLIDAYS

It should be made quite clear whether or not the organist is responsible for finding a deputy during his holidays. An organist may also feel that the choir should have the month of August off—if, of course, the choir itself does not object to this.*

WEDDINGS

A figure should be agreed upon, and there should be some definite payment for choirchildren (under sixteen), teenagers (sixteen–twenty-one), and adults.

* This may sound strange, but some loyal choir members, finding themselves at home during August, very much miss their church choir.

158

While the organist is discussing the question of money (i.e. before he takes up his appointment) he may find it the best moment to ask for a definite annual sum for the purchase of new music for the choir library, and the renewal of hymn books, etc., as they inevitably collapse under the strain of continual use. He might also ask for an occasional allowance (provided that the size of the congregation warrants it) for a few instrumentalists to perform in small cantatas; e.g. an oboe for "Jesu, joy of man's desiring" (J. S. Bach), or an occasional string quartet, or a couple of trumpets, for an important occasion. Money will also be needed for the choir outing. The terms of the organist's appointment should be included in an agreement in writing, and not merely be the subject of a verbal agreement.

OFFICIAL BODIES

THE ROYAL SCHOOL OF CHURCH MUSIC

This is a body which gives a great deal of help in matters of Church music.

The School of English Church Music was established in 1927 by Dr. (afterwards Sir Sydney) Nicholson, with the support and approval of the Church Music Society (see page 161). The object of the S.E.C.M. was the improvement of Anglican Church music, and by 1939 over 1,500 church choirs had become affiliated to it.

In 1929 the S.E.C.M. founded a training centre for the study of Anglican Church music—the College of St. Nicholas. This was originally at Chislehurst, then at Canterbury, and finally at Addington Palace, Croydon (1954 to the present time).

In 1945, by Royal Command, the S.E.C.M. became the Royal School of Church Music. Today, about 7,500 churches and schools in all six continents are affiliated to the R.S.C.M. About half of the many men and women students, from all parts of the Anglican Communion, come to Addington Palace from overseas—mainly from the British Commonwealth and the United States of America. The present Director of the R.S.C.M. is Dr. Gerald H. Knight.

At Addington Palace church musicians receive specialised instruction in plainsong, organ, harmony and counterpoint, aural training and liturgiology, as well as practical experience in training choirs and in accompanying services.

Candidates for graduate degrees and diplomas (Mus.Bac., F.R.C.O., A.R.C.O., A.R.C.M., etc.) normally take a three years' residential course at Addington Palace. Students are also accepted for a one year's specialised course in Church music, and there is sometimes accommodation for those who wish to make use of the facilities which the Palace offers (including the Colles library, which houses one of the finest collections of Church music in existence). All resident students take an active part in the chapel services and choir practices; most students are members of the Anglican Communion, but members of other denominations are accepted.

Communicant members of the Church of England (or of Churches in communion therewith) who have obtained both the Fellowship and the Choir-Training Diploma of the Royal College of Organists, are eligible to enter for the examination for the Archbishop of Canterbury's Diploma in Church Music (A.D.C.M.), the highest award available to musicians in the Church of England. Candidates require a sound knowledge of the Liturgy and of Church music from 1550 onwards, and a detailed study of a special subject (e.g. "Plainsong and its accompaniment").

There are short refresher courses (a half-day, a weekend or longer) for organists, choirmasters, ordinands, the junior clergy, readers, schoolteachers, and adult or boy singers in choirs. These courses (held at Addington Palace and at other centres) are open to resident or non-resident students. Some courses are intended for those taking the Choir-Training and Diploma examinations of the Royal College of Organists, and the Archbishop of Canterbury's Certificate in Church Music (see page 162).

On most Saturdays during full term, choirs affiliated to the R.S.C.M. visit Addington Palace to sing Evensong in the Chapel of St. Nicholas, and choirmasters are invited to be present as observers.

An important part of the R.S.C.M.'s activities is the work of the publication department, which publishes books and study notes on many aspects of Church music, as well as choir and service books, anthems, services, hymns, and such things as choir registers, service sheets, etc. The publication department is also able to supply any book on music issued by a publisher in the U.K.

A prospectus giving details of the courses, and a list of R.S.C.M. publications, may be had from The Warden, Addington Palace, Croydon, Surrey.

THE CHURCH MUSIC SOCIETY

This Society was founded in 1906, at a time when the music available to church choirs was in urgent need of improvement. With the Bishop of Stepney, Cosmo Lang (afterwards Archbishop Lord Lang) as President and (Sir) Henry Hadow as Chairman, the Society attracted eager support.

The aim of the Society has always been "to facilitate the selection and performance of the music which is most suitable for different occasions of divine worship, and for choirs of varying powers". In its early days the Society found it necessary to publish cheap editions of works not otherwise available; these included Bach's "Jesu, joy of man's desiring" which was published for the first time in England, with a translation of the words made specially for the Society by Dr. Robert Bridges.

A series of "Occasional" and "Shorter" papers was also inaugurated, the first Occasional paper *The Need for Reform in Church Music* being written by Fuller Maitland, editor of the second edition of *Grove's Dictionary of Music and Musicians*. The Society also publishes a number of anthems and services (obtainable from the Oxford University Press), many of which have gone out of print in other editions. In 1951 the Society assisted with a substantial grant the publication of the Archbishop's Report *Music in Church*, and in 1963 it offered a scholarship, tenable at the Royal School of Church Music, to a student from overseas.

The Honorary Secretary and Treasurer of the Society is Mrs. E. T. Cook, Southwark Cottage, Howe Green, Chipstead, Surrey.

INCORPORATED GUILD OF CHURCH MUSICIANS

This Guild, founded in 1888, and originally known as the Church Choir Guild, exists to raise the technical and general knowledge and proficiency of Anglican Church musicians, and to help and encourage members to study and enter for the Archbishop of Canterbury's Certificate in Church Music. Membership is open to members of the Church of England, together with other Churches in communion with Canterbury, who have an interest in Church music.

The Archbishop of Canterbury's Certificate in Church Music is open (*a*) to organists and choirmasters, and (*b*) to singers. Candidates, who must be members of the Guild, are examined at approved centres in July of each year. The examination is in four parts, any of which may be taken separately; but the whole examination must be completed within a period of three years. The requirements are listed below.

	Organists/Choirmasters	*Singers*
Part 1	Practical Organ Playing	Practical Singing
Part 2	Choir Training and Organ Accompaniment	Practical Singing in Church
Part 3	Prayer Book	Prayer Book
Part 4	History of Church Music	History of Church Music

To qualify for Part 1, candidates must submit evidence that, during the previous ten years, they have passed one of the grade examinations, not below Grade V, of the Associated Board, Trinity College of Music, etc. Candidates who hold diplomas (Performer or Teacher) in organ or pianoforte, or in singing, may claim exemption from this part. The examiners for Parts 2 and 4 are appointed by the Incorporated Guild of Church Musicians, and for Part 3 by the Archbishop of Canterbury, to whom successful candidates are presented to receive their certificates.

The Guild Council has recently introduced a preliminary examination for organists and choirmasters. Candidates, who receive certificates if successful, are required to answer elementary questions on the rudiments of music, the quality and pitch of organ stops, and the service of Holy Communion, Mattins or Evensong; to detect wrong notes in the melody of a four-part hymn or double-chant played by the examiner; to perform a prepared piece for manuals only; and to read a simple hymn tune at sight (pedals optional).

The General Secretary of the Incorporated Guild of Church Musicians is Mr. Douglas Coates, 7 Tufton Street, London, S.W.1; the Registrar and Examinations Secretary is Mr. A. J. Pinder, 16 The Cloisters, Windsor Castle, Berks.

This Association was established in 1955 with the approval of the late Cardinal Griffin, with the object of concerning itself with all aspects of the music of the Roman Catholic Church in the light of the Papal Encyclicals and other documents dealing with the subject.

The Association holds a residential course in sacred music each year during Low Week, covering the needs of choirmasters, organists, choir singers, and those responsible for music in Roman Catholic schools. Short courses (a day or a weekend) are also arranged from time to time, and there is a series of lectures in London in conjunction with the Evening Institutes. The Association awards certificates to choirmasters and organists who satisfy the examiners of their competence; the standard required is that which is considered adequate for an ordinary parish church. Choir Festivals and Adjudications are also held in different centres throughout the country. The association has established its own publishing company, St. Martins Publications Ltd. Membership of the Association is open to individuals, and to groups (choirs, etc.). The address of the Office is 48 Great Peter Street, Westminster, London, S.W.1.

THE METHODIST CHURCH MUSIC SOCIETY

Formed in 1935, this is a fellowship of organists, choirmasters, choristers, ministers, and all others interested in the cause of the music of the Methodist Church. The organisation of the Society is on the official Methodist pattern—the Connexional Committee appointed by Conference, the District Committee and the Circuit Committee. The annual conference is held in October, and district festivals (as well as festivals at Circuit level) are held at frequent intervals. Membership may be personal for individuals, or corporate for choirs. Further information may be obtained from The Ministerial Secretary, Methodist Church Music Society, 1 Central Buildings, Westminster, London, S.W.1.

THE GUILD OF CONGREGATIONAL ORGANISTS AND CHOIRMASTERS

This Guild was founded in 1951 by the Revd. Erik Routley, D.Phil., F.R.S.C.M., then lecturer in Church History and Director of Music at Mansfield College, Oxford. It was open to all who served Congregational Churches in music, and in that year held its first conference at Mansfield College, which set the pattern for annual conferences thereafter. The conference was held over a summer weekend, and was designed to provide the opportunity for worship, fellowship and study. Conferences were held at the College until 1957, and in 1959, 1961, 1963 and 1965: in the other years, other places were visited. Dr. Routley resigned the leadership of the Guild when he left Oxford in 1959, and his successor is Mr. Peter Cutts. His address is 58 Rawthorpe Lane, Dalton, Huddersfield, during term; at other times, 94 Penns Lane, Sutton Coldfield, Warwickshire.

A local Guild was formed in Surrey in 1960 (The Guild of Surrey Congregational Organists and Choirmasters); the Secretary is Mr. David Wilson, 18 Guildford Park Avenue, Guildford, Surrey.

THE FREE CHURCH CHOIR UNION

This Union was founded in 1888, with the object of arranging annual meetings and choral festivals, so that Nonconformist musicians from all parts of the country could be brought together for a common purpose. Many large-scale festivals were given at the Crystal Palace, and choral competitions for choirs (and composers) were inaugurated.

Today the main work of the Union consists in helping choirs to get together to perform oratorios and sacred music which the smaller choir cannot render. An annual Festival Service of Church Music is held (usually at the City Temple), and a festival music book is published containing the anthems at the festival service. These anthem books should prove most useful to choirmasters of many denominations. The Union also holds a one-day course for choir leaders and members, and a competition for anthem, hymn tune, chant composition, or for the words of a hymn.

The President of the Union is Dr. Eric Thiman, the Hon. General Secretary Mr. Alan A. Neubert, 1 and 2 Old Cottages, Leaves Green, Keston, Kent, and the Treasurer (from whom the anthem books may be obtained) Mr. James Findlay, "Glengariff", 2 Hill Crest, Sevenoaks, Kent.

THE BAPTIST MUSIC SOCIETY

This Society was formed in 1961, with the object of raising the standard of musical taste and performance in the worship of

Baptist Churches by providing training courses for organists and choir members in various parts of the country (directed both by Baptist musicians and others including Drs. Harold Darke, Francis Jackson, Erik Routley and Eric Thiman), and by the publication of a periodical newsletter, giving advice on Church music and musical instruments.

The Society also sponsored a festival service to celebrate the publication of the new *Baptist Hymn Book* in March, 1962.

Personal membership is open to ministers and organists at a nominal subscription. Choirs may join as Group Members, and others as Associate Members. The Chairman is Mr. Gerald L. Barnes, F.R.C.O., G.R.S.M., Bloomsbury Central Church, Shaftesbury Avenue, London, W.C.2; the Secretary, Mr. David Lovegrove, 9 Endsleigh Gardens, London, W.C.1; and the Treasurer, Miss P. E. Merriman, M.A., F.I.A., 28 Nassington Road, London, N.W.3.

THE PLAINSONG AND MEDIAEVAL MUSIC SOCIETY

The object with which this Society was founded (in 1888) was that "of encouraging the study and performance both of the Gregorian chant and of 'Mediaeval Music' in the sense of that European music, choral or instrumental, which lay behind the flowering of the Tudor period".

The Society (with Dr. Herbert Howells now President, and the Revd. Dom Anselm Hughes Chairman of the Council) is primarily antiquarian in basis, and is not restricted to any particular religious denomination. The Society has published facsimile volumes of original manuscripts of medieval music, critical performing editions of works such as *The Old Hall Manuscript* and *Worcester Mediaeval Harmony*, books and pamphlets for study, and reliable choir texts (all available to the general public through the Faith Press).

The Society is a centre of information and communication for students of plainsong and medieval music who live in or out of this country; members have free access to the Society's extensive library (which includes early printed books, and text books of all periods) at the Royal College of Organists in London.

The present Secretary is Mr. Charles Colhoun, c/o Lloyd's Bank, 112–114 Kensington High Street, London, W.8.

THE GREGORIAN ASSOCIATION

In 1870, as a result of a meeting of Churchmen convened "to consider what steps should be taken to improve the choral portions of the services of the Church", the London Gregorian Association was founded. In 1912 the name was changed to The Gregorian Association. The objects of the Association are to spread reliable information on plainsong and to promote its use; to demonstrate its suitability to the Anglican rite and to combat prejudice against it by the holding of an annual festival in St. Paul's Cathedral and in other cathedrals and churches (the music of these services being published as a handbook), and by lectures and conferences; and to afford expert advice and instruction to those desiring to introduce plainsong into parishes and schools. Some Church music is also published, and may be purchased from Novello & Co. The Hon. General Secretary of The Gregorian Association is Mr. R. J. Dabner, "Carolus", 67 Grange Crescent, Grange Hill, Chigwell, Essex.

THE GUILD OF ST. GREGORY

The Guild exists to help organists, choirmasters and adult choristers in their spiritual lives, and to promote and to encourage the study and use of plainchant. Membership is confined to communicant members of the Church of England who pledge themselves to observe the precepts of the Church, and are actively engaged in Church or are students of liturgy.

A choir is maintained which sings Evensong on Tuesdays and mid-day Mass on Fridays at the City Church of St. Mary, Aldermay (near Mansion House station). Enquiries regarding membership and Guild publications should be addressed to the Hon. Secretary, Mr. W. J. D. Gardner, 1 Marlborough Road, Luton, Beds.

SCOTTISH EPISCOPAL CHURCH MUSIC COMMITTEE

This committee exists to promote and improve Church music in the province of the Episcopal Church in Scotland, working in close co-operation with the Royal School of Church Music. The Secretary is The Provost of St. Andrew's Cathedral, Aberdeen (The Very Revd. A. E. Hodgkinson).

THE HYMN SOCIETY OF GREAT BRITAIN AND IRELAND

This Society was founded in 1936 with the objects (1) to bring together for co-operative study, research and fellowship those who have been concerned in the preparation and revision of hymn books, with all others who are interested in the subject; (2) to continue and to bring up-to-date the work begun by Dr. Julian and his collaborators in the *Dictionary of Hymnology*; (3) to foster a spirit of catholic unity among all Christian communions in the field of hymnody; (4) to raise the standard of hymns, both words and music, in churches, colleges and schools, to promote their more reverent and understanding use in worship, and to encourage the study of hymnology in the theological colleges and elsewhere; (5) to publish from time to time information which may be useful to members and advance the study of hymnology.

A conference is held, usually each year, for the discussion of the Society's business, and the normal practice is to provide lectures or public hymn singing for the furtherance of its ideals among the Christian public.

The *Bulletin* (Hon. Editor the Revd. Erik Routley) is published three or four times a year. A revised and abridged volume of Julian's *Dictionary of Hymnology* is being prepared (1966) by the Revd. L. H. Bunn. The Society (whose present membership stands at about three hundred) keeps in close touch with The Hymn Society of America (founded in 1922), particularly with regard to the revision of *Julian*.

The Hon. Secretary of The Hymn Society is the Revd. Wilfred J. Little, Ash Tree House, Audlem, Crewe, Cheshire.

THE INCORPORATED ASSOCIATION OF ORGANISTS

Founded in 1913, this is an Organists' Fellowship which meets for one week in August each year at a different place in Great Britain for lectures, discussions and recitals, and also publishes an official periodical. Affiliated to this Association is The Scottish Societies of Organists which was formed in 1957 to bring together for one Saturday in each year the various societies of organists in Scotland. The Hon. General Secretary of The Incorporated Association of Organists is Mr. George Galloway, F.R.C.O. (CHM), L.R.A.M., A.R.C.M., 66 Swinley Road, Wigan, Lancashire.

LONDON ASSOCIATION OF ORGANISTS

This Association (founded in 1961) has for its objects the improvement and advancement of the profession of organists and choirmasters by arranging conferences, lectures, recitals, etc., and by publishing a Bulletin. There are a number of associated societies in different parts of London. The Hon. Secretary is Mr. Bernard Honess, 28 Bushey Way, Park Langley, Beckenham, Kent.

THE ORGAN CLUB

The Organ Club, which was inaugurated in 1926, is a society of enthusiasts for the organ. The aim and object of this non-profit-making club is the creation and fostering of individual and public interest in the organ, and the increased appreciation of organ music.

The Organ Club promotes monthly meetings, mainly (but not exclusively) in the London area, to see, hear and try good organs and those of special technical interest; these include pipe organs of every style and period, whether in cathedral, church, concert hall, cinema or residence. Electronic instruments, in the style of pipe organs, are not excluded.

Lectures and organ recitals are arranged from time to time, and there is usually a visit to an organ-builder's works each year. The Club has a fine library (housed at The Royal College of Organists) of over three hundred books, including many technical treatises on organ construction. *The Organ Club Journal*, which is published about six times a year, is sent to all members. Membership enquiries should be addressed to the Hon. Membership Secretary, 31 Clatterfield Gardens, Westcliff-on-Sea, Essex.

CHOIR SCHOOLS

For a boy with a musical voice, a choir school is the obvious choice as the first place of education. The Choir Schools' Association publishes annually *The Choir Schools Directory* (obtainable from the Hon. Secretary, Mr. B. J. Rushby Smith, Minster Grammar School, Southwell, Notts.). This directory contains information about the conditions of entry to nearly forty choir schools, the advantages which are offered by each, and the dates of voice trials. These schools include the cathedral choir schools at St. Paul's, Westminster, Canterbury, etc., and such famous choir schools as St. Michael's College, Tenbury, and St. George's School, Windsor Castle, as well as The Cathedral Choir School, New York, and St. Andrew's Cathedral School, Sydney.

One school which is not to be found in the directory is St. Mary-of-the-Angels Song School, Crabtrees, Long Bottom Lane, Seer Green, Nr. Beaconsfield, Bucks. This Anglo-Catholic song school was founded some forty years ago by the Revd. Desmond Morse-Boycott and his wife. At first intended to train boys from the slum areas as singing boys, the school developed into a choir school for boys of all classes; it is a charitable trust living from hand to mouth, as the Church of England has never given it official recognition. The "Angels", as the choirboys are known locally, have sung in thousands of churches and halls at home and abroad, and have appeared on television and in many films. The boys, who are selected by recommendation, must have passable voices, and a love of the Church; the song school has already produced more than twenty priests.

CHORAL EXCHANGE SCHEME

Organists may or may not be aware of a very good scheme run by the National Federation of Music Societies (4 St. James's Square, London, S.W.1) called a "Choral Exchange Scheme". Choirs belonging to this pay an annual subscription, and are entitled to borrow music from other choirs who have sent lists of the music they have available on loan to this central body. A small hiring fee is payable by agreement between the two choirs concerned.

CHAPTER NINE

PATTERNS OF RITUAL IN SERVICES

In a book of this size it is possible to attempt only a brief summary of ritual* in the commoner services in weekly use in Churches of various denominations. Because of the many variations in ritual between different churches of the same denomination, it is only possible to describe the basic patterns, and principally from the music angle. Patterns (1967) are changing fast; some parts of this chapter may soon be out of date.

THE CHURCH OF ENGLAND

In parish churches Holy Communion, Mattins and Evensong are the official forms of Sunday worship. In many churches, however, the Parish Communion (at about 9 a.m. on Sunday) is the principal service of the day. At this, the sung Eucharist is followed by a sermon and the communion of all the congregation. Mattins will then probably be said at an earlier hour; it is sometimes sung at about 11 a.m., and may be followed by an additional service of Communion. In churches with Protestant (or Low) traditions the pattern may differ from those with Anglo-Catholic (or High) traditions, as may the names of the services. Thus, in Anglo-Catholic churches the Holy Communion (or Eucharist) may be called Sung Mass, High Mass or Low Mass, the order of these services very nearly following that of the Roman Mass (q.v.). Likewise, Evensong may become Solemn Evensong, Sermon and Devotions.

THE EUCHARIST (OR HOLY COMMUNION)
The table on pages 172 and 174 represents the service in its traditional shape in an average Church of England church, a tradition

* *Ritual* is, properly, what is said, and *Ceremonial* what is done; ritual is used here to indicate the two together.

170

which may be described as the Prayer Book Liturgy.* Little booklets like *A Parish Communion Book* by R. R. Roseveare, Bishop of Accra (Mowbray), or *The Service of Holy Communion with the Melody of Merbecke* (S.P.C.K.), enables members of the congregation and choir to participate actively. There are, of course, many settings other than Merbecke's of a simple nature which a congregation can soon learn.

The table on pages 173 and 175 represents the modifications in a church with an Anglo-Catholic tradition; the "Traditional Liturgy", as found in the *English Missal*. The music for this can be found in *The English Gradual* by Francis Burgess, published by Plainchant Publications Committee, c/o 23 Lichfield Road, Datchet, Berks. Part 1 is the Ordinary (or unchanging part of the service): Part 2 is the Proper (or variable part). The right-hand column is, in essence, a simplified English translation of the Roman Catholic Mass (the music is also simpler), and all the remarks in Burgess's book about two *Alleluyas* on Eastertide, and so on, correspond exactly with the Roman Catholic ritual.

There are a few essential differences between the order of the Church of England and Roman Catholic services. They are worth tabulating.

(1) *Gloria in Excelsis*. Church of England, near the end: Roman Catholic, near the beginning.

(2) *Sermon and Notices*. Church of England, after the creed: Roman Catholic before the creed (after the Gospel).

(3) *The Lord's Prayer*. Church of England, after the Communion: Roman Catholic, before *Agnus Dei* (i.e. before the Communion).

(4) *Postcommunion*. Roman Catholic only, after the Communion.

(5) *Prayer for King's Majesty*. Roman Catholic and Anglo-Catholic tradition.

(6) *Other slight differences*. Church of England has no *Alleluia*, Tract or Sequence, Motet, Prayer over offerings, Canon, etc. But these are smaller differences, rather in the form of omissions.

* The Church of England Liturgical Commission's *Alternative Services* (Second Series, 1966) is published by S.P.C.K. The alterations are possibly as far-reaching as those of the 1928 Prayer Book.

EUCHARIST (*Prayer Book Liturgy**)

(*People* = Choir and people.   *Choir* = Choir only.)

Opening or processional hymn (1)
Prayers (Lord's Prayer, Collect for Purity) spoken.

Ninefold Kyrie OR	*Commandments* OR	*Shortened Commandments*
(*People*)	(*Priest*)	(*Priest*)
Kyrie Eleison	The ten command-	The two "basic"
(Lord have mercy	ments spoken or	commandments, spoken
upon us.)	intoned.	or intoned.
(3 times)	(*People*)	(*People*)
Christe Eleison	Lord have mercy	Lord have mercy upon
(Christ have mercy	upon us, and write	us, and incline our
upon us.)	all these laws in our	hearts to keep this
(3 times)	hearts we beseech	law.
Kyrie Eleison	thee.	
(Lord have mercy		
upon us.)		
(3 times)		

Collect(s)
Epistle (usually read)
Gradual Hymn (2)
The Gospel (intoned or spoken)
   (*Priest intones*): The Holy Gospel . . . beginning at the . . . verse.
   (*People:*) Glory be to thee O Lord.
   After the Gospel:
   (*People:*) Praise be to thee O Christ.
Creed
   (*Priest:*) I believe in one God.
   (*People:*) The Father Almighty, Maker, etc.
Sermon
Offertory sentence
Offertory hymn (3)
Notices (or before Sermon)
Prayers
Sursum Corda (Lift up your hearts) Responses sung between Priest
   and People.
The Preface (*Priest*) ending . . . evermore praising Thee and saying.
Sanctus (*People*) Holy, Holy, Holy. . .

[*continued on p. 174*

* This might be described as "average Church of England".

HOLY COMMUNION

EUCHARIST (*Traditional Liturgy**)

Introit Proper. Introit: psalm verse: *Gloria: Introit* repeated (*Gloria* omitted in Passiontide). Sarum custom adds another *Introit* after the psalm verse.
Kyrie Eleison (Lord have mercy, etc.).
Gloria in Excelsis Deo (Glory be to God on high).

Collect(s)
Epistle (may be intoned)
Gradual Proper. Verses from Scripture (usually sung alternately by cantors and choir).
Alleluia or *Tract* follows immediately. (Organists are advised not to modulate from the *Gradual* to the first note of the *Alleluia*. A short pause is sufficient.)
Sequence occurs on a few Feast Days.
     The above pattern, *Gradual-Alleluia-Sequence*, varies throughout the year, but the variations are made quite clear in the "English Gradual". They are also explained fully in the Catholic Mass. (Sarum custom: omit the amens at the end of the *Sequence*, and proceed immediately to the final *Alleluia*.)
The Gospel (may be intoned)
     (Same responses)
Sermon
The Nicene Creed
Offertory Proper. Sung while the offertory is recited at the altar. More verses from Scripture (intoned as before). While the Priest incenses the Oblations and Altar, and while he and all present are incensed, an anthem or hymn may be sung.

[*continued on p. 175*

* This might be described as "High Church".

Benedictus (*People or Men only*) Blessed is he . . . (sometimes omitted).
Prayers
Agnus Dei (*Choir*) O Lamb of God. Three phrases sung while bread
and wine are being prepared (sometimes omitted).
The Communion
Hymn (4), or hymns, or anthem(s) may be sung softly during the
Communion, or the organ may play; silence is also very effective.
Lord's Prayer (sung or spoken by all)
Gloria in Excelsis.
(*Priest:*) Glory be to God on High.
(*People:*) And in earth peace, etc.
Blessing.
Closing or Recessional Hymn (5) (also called "Hymn at the ablu-
tions").

CHORAL EUCHARIST

In this the italicised portions of the table on pages 172 and 174 are
often sung to Merbecke's setting (1550); there are also other
settings. All of the italicised portions may be spoken; none of the
five hymns are an essential part of the service (please note: none
of the remarks "usually read", etc., need be taken in any sense
as binding; these are common practices today (1967) in many
Church of England churches). Christ Himself said little about the
form services should take.

Accompaniments to Merbecke's setting of the Eucharist are
published (1) by O.U.P. (accompaniment by J. H. Arnold);
(2) by the Faith Press (accompaniment by Sydney H. Nicholson).
This last, although it supplies possible harmonies, muddles the
plainsong rhythm with minims and crotchets and various dotted
rhythms. These are best ignored. Provided an organist has a good
grasp of chords I, II, III, IV, V and VI in root position and first
inversion, he would do much better to invent his own harmonic
accompaniment, placing chords under the natural stresses; (3) by
Novello (accompaniment by Royle Shore); (4) by S.P.C.K.
(accompaniment by Eric Hunt and Gerald Knight).

Other settings of the Holy Communion which may be suitable
for many parish churches include Martin Shaw's *Simple Setting*,
Modal Setting and *Anglican Folk Mass* (Curwen); C. Hylton
Stewart's *Office for the Holy Communion* (S.P.C.K.), set to simple

The secret prayer(s)
The Preface
Sanctus
Canon of the Mass — Consecration of the Host — Consecration of the Chalice.
Lord's Prayer
Agnus Dei
Communion Proper begins immediately after the *Agnus Dei*. More verses from Scripture with *Alleluias*.
Post Communion prayer(s)
Blessing
Prayer for the Queen — responses — spoken prayer — amen. Said at the conclusion of the principal service on every Sunday in the year.

phrases for voices in unison, and intended for congregational singing; and the simple plainsong settings of the Ordinary of the Mass (Plainsong and Mediaeval Music Society). There is also an interesting Communion Service by Kenneth Leighton, in a simple modern setting, which can be sung in unison or harmony at the Parish Eucharist (Church Music Society–O.U.P.).

The priest's music for the prefaces and during the Communion, together with a key to plainchant notation is published by The Plainchant Publications Committee (see page 171); it is called *The Ritual Music of the Prefaces,* and is edited by Francis Burgess. This Committee also publishes a number of liturgical music and choir books.

J. H. Arnold's *Priest's Music for the Liturgy* (O.U.P.) gives all the chants for the *Sursum Corda,* with much other information for the clergy.

THE CONFIRMATION SERVICE

Although this is a distinct Rite, it usually takes place before the Communion Service, or after the sermon as the Bishop may direct. When there is no Eucharist, the service may start with a hymn to the Holy Spirit. The laying-on of hands may take place in silence or, if the candidates are very numerous, one or two short hymns or anthems may be sung.

Opening hymn—or introit (there is no authority for this in the Prayer Book (1662 or 1928), but it is a common practice).

Versicles and responses (sometimes starting with "O Lord open thou", etc.).

Venite (Psalm 95), often first seven verses only.

An "Office" hymn is sometimes inserted here.

Psalm(s) (see note at foot of "Evensong", page 177).

First lesson (Old Testament).

Te Deum or *Benedicite* (the *Te Deum* has no *Gloria*, and may sometimes end at "Make them to be numbered", etc.).

Second lesson (New Testament).

Benedictus or *Jubilate Deo* (Psalm 100).

(If the Eucharist is to follow, Mattins may end here with the Second and Third Collects, followed by "The Grace of our Lord", etc.)

Creed and responses (including a second Lord's Prayer, sometimes omitted). Both the Creed and the Lord's Prayer may be said or sung.

Intoned collects with sung amens.

Anthem, or hymn.

Hymn (may be omitted if anthem is long, or is replaced by a hymn).

⎰Prayers (Sometimes omitted if separate Eucharist is to follow
⎱Hymn   Mattins.)

Sermon.

Blessing and amen.

Hymn (possibly a recessional hymn).

EVENSONG

Opening hymn (not if there is an "Office" hymn*).

Versicles and responses (sometimes starting with "O Lord open thou", etc.).

(An Office hymn is sometimes inserted here—alternatively, it may be sung between the First Lesson and the *Magnificat*.)

Psalm(s).

First lesson (Old Testament).

---

* The "Office" hymn should be objective, bearing upon the service of the day. At Mattins and Evensong it should, strictly speaking, be introduced immediately before the Psalms; in some churches, at Evensong, it is sung just before the *Magnificat*.

Magnificat or *Cantate Domino.*
Second lesson (New Testament).
Nunc Dimittis or *Deus Misereatur.*
From this point as for Mattins.

The psalms, sung on Sundays and Holy Days, used to be according to the day of the month (i.e. if it was Mattins on April 10th, Psalms 50–52 were available). It is more common practice today to select the psalm according to the particular feast—details are available in the *Churchman's Kalendar* (Mowbray). The list given in the 1928 Prayer Book is more commonly used.

THE LITANY

Litany (from the Greek) means a prayer or supplication. The English Litany was designed by Archbishop Cranmer who, in 1544, adapted the music of the Latin Litany to English words. The Litany was intended to be sung in procession, with hymns and responses, the congregation standing or kneeling. The 1928 revision of the Prayer Book directs that the Litany be used on Rogation Days, and "at other times when it shall be commanded by the Ordinary". In many parish churches the Litany is an occasional service, sometimes said, sometimes sung in procession or otherwise; sometimes it is followed immediately by the Eucharist, when it may end at the *Kyrie* before the Lord's Prayer, which then opens the Eucharist service. The music of Cranmer's Litany was originally sung in unison, but there are many harmonised versions; those edited by E. H. Fellowes and S. H. Nicholson (Faith Press) are more attractive than Stainer's four-part harmonisation in the *Cathedral Prayer Book* (Nov., 1891); a fine plainsong setting *The Litany set to the Chant of the Sarum Processional* is published for the Church Music Society by O.U.P. The Litany set to plainsong is also in the *Manual of Plainsong*, edited by Briggs and Frere, revised and enlarged by J. H. Arnold (Nov.).

In the Episcopal Church of Scotland (which is a province of the Anglican Church), the second Shorter Litany is now widely used in place of the Prayer for the Whole State of Christ's Church (in the Scottish Prayer Book of 1929); the music for this was produced privately by Patrick Shannon (late Provost of St. Andrew's Cathedral, Aberdeen), and is used in many Scottish Episcopal Churches. Copies can be obtained from the present Provost.

BAPTISM

So that a baptism may be witnessed by a large number of Christians, the Prayer Book orders that it should be administered at Mattins or Evensong (often after the third Collect): an amen is then sometimes added in the middle of the service, or the hymn "God be in his/her head" may be sung.

If the baptism service is conducted by itself, it is usually without music. Baptisms may also take place at the Parish Communion.

WEDDINGS

The incumbent has the sole right to permit the use of music at weddings. If hymns are included, they are better sung before and after the service. If a choir is present, they should be in their places before the bride arrives at the church.*

Music before the bride arrives (say, ten–fifteen minutes).

Entry processional music (e.g. Wagner's *Lohengrin*), or the bride can enter to the singing of a hymn. In some churches the choir precedes the bride in the procession.

Psalm (while the bride and bridegroom move up to the altar); or sometimes a metrical version of a psalm (this is not an *authorised* practice).

If the bride and bridegroom make their first Communion together, most of the Communion Service might be inserted here: the previous psalm then serves as an introit for the Communion.

Possibly another hymn.

During the signing of the register, the choir may sing one (or more) anthems, or the organist may play.

The Wedding March (e.g. Mendelssohn).

Organists are often asked if there are alternatives to the Wagner and Mendelssohn wedding marches; there is no obligation to have them! Here is a suggested list; there are many others.

Widor, *Toccata* from Symphony No. 5 (U.M.P.).
Purcell, *Trumpet Tune and Air*, arr. Peasgood (Nov.).
Boellmann, *Toccata* from *Gothic Suite* (Ashdown).
Grieg, *Triumphal March*, Op. 56, No. 3, arr. R. Groves (Peters).

* The *Choral Wedding Service Book* (R.S.C.M.) contains the Wedding Service, two musical settings of the versicles and responses, three psalms, and a selection of twenty-one hymns.

Handel, *Arrival of the Queen of Sheba (Solomon)*, arr. Archer (Paxton).

Bach. Any of the festive preludes and fugues, e.g. Prelude (and Fugue) in C Major (Vol. III, ed. Bridge and Higgs) (Nov.).

Parry, *Bridal March (Birds of Aristophanes)*, arr. Alcock (Nov.).

J. Clarke, *Trumpet Voluntary*, arr. D. Ratcliffe (Nov.).

Stanley, *Trumpet Voluntary* (4th movement of a sonata) (O.U.P.).

FUNERALS

If music is used, a typical form of service is as follows:

Music as the congregation assembles. This may continue softly as the coffin is brought in and the priest says the opening sentences.

While the priest reads a psalm (e.g. 23), the organ might play very softly, though this is not looked upon with great favour by purists; speaking across music being considered "theatrical" or "American".

Lesson.

Prayers.

At a cremation: The Committal (soft music during this).

Prayer and blessing.

Music as the congregation disperses.

(An album of memorial and funeral marches is published by O.U.P., and an album of wedding and funeral marches by Joseph Williams.)

NINE LESSONS AND CAROLS

This service (often held in place of Evensong on the Sunday before, or the Sunday after, Christmas Day) has recently become very popular, although it is not an official service of the Church of England. Some ministers consider it more correct to sing carols *after* Christmas. The carols should ideally fit either the lesson they precede or the lesson they follow, and there should be enough carols for both choir and congregation. The lessons have traditionally become: (1) Genesis 3: 8–15; (2) Genesis 22: 15–18; (3) Isaiah 9: 2, 6, 7; (4) Isaiah 11: 1–9, *or* Micah 5: 2–4; (5) St. Luke 1: 26–33 and 38, *or* Isaiah 60: 1–6 and 19; (6) St. Matthew 1: 18–23, *or* St. Luke 2: 1–7; (8) St. Matthew 1: 1–11, *or* St. Matthew 2: 9–12; (9) St. John 1: 1–14.

But the organist should remember that a processional hymn is needed to begin with (e.g. "Once in Royal David's City"), and there may also be a "Bidding" when the priest opens the service; so that the service might begin as follows:

Processional hymn
Bidding
Carol
First lesson.

After this point, lesson alternates with carol (or two carols may be used—one for the congregation, one for the choir) until the final lesson (usually read by the vicar). The service may end as follows:

Ninth lesson
Carol (or hymn) for collection
Prayers—blessing
Recessional hymn.

The Lessons may be read by a choirboy, a choirgirl, a choirman, a member of the congregation, a churchwarden, a server, a bell-ringer, the organist, the assistant priest, the priest in charge, a Sunday School teacher, etc.

COMPLINE

A less used form of service for late evening, short and rather beautiful. This includes responses, certain selected psalms, the hymn "Before the ending of the day", the *Nunc Dimittis*, the Creed, and other responses. There is a pamphlet produced by the Plainsong and Mediaeval Music Society called *An order for Compline* (Faith Press). The order is also in the 1928 Prayer Book.

SCHOOL SERVICES

These tend to build up a shape of their own, and conditions vary according to the size and type of school. A boy's public school may have a large or small choir (with masters helping to augment the tenors and basses). In other schools where there are only unison choirs, good antiphonal effects are possible when plainsong is sung; the use of descants also lends interest to the singing of hymns. When, as in some schools, there is no choir, the music to be sung will need to be simple and familiar. A weekly practice for the whole school is, however, essential if good singing is to be aimed at. On occasions interest may be added if hymns are accompanied by the school orchestra, a brass band, or recorders, as well as the conventional piano or organ.*

THE MASS

The Mass is the chief act of worship in the Roman rite. At the present date there is a great deal of discussion and revision going on, and in fact some of the details mentioned in this book may be out of date by the time it is printed. For example, the service has been hitherto spoken or sung in Latin in all countries, but today the vernacular is also being used—sometimes concurrently with Latin. Some simple plainsong is also being used, and there is a tendency to make more use of hymns—especially at Low Mass.

The Mass is found in three different forms:

(1) *Solemn High Mass* (*Missa Solemnis*), the most impressive performance of the Mass, is carried out by the celebrant (who actually offers the Mass), and by the deacon and sub-deacon (who sing parts of the liturgy).

(2) *Sung Mass* (*Missa Cantata*), a more simple service with one priest, who sings all suitable parts of the Mass.

(3) *Low Mass* (*Missa Cum Cantu*), in which the celebrant does not sing any parts. There may be as many hymns as possible (especially Gélineau Psalms) sung by the choir, generally in these places:

Introit/Offertory/Communion (several hymns if necessary)/*Recessional.*

The *Kyrie*, *Gloria*, etc., may be sung in plainsong, with cantors and the choir singing alternate verses.

Most Roman Catholic churches have at least some sort of a choir; but if there should be no choir, as a rule there is no Sung Mass (*Missa Solemnis* or *Missa Cantata*). The Mass would then be spoken by the priest (Low Mass).

The Mass has two parts—the *Ordinary* (or invariable parts) and the *Proper* (or variable parts, changing from day to day, or feast to feast). The *Proper* consists of the *Introit, Collects, Epistle, Gradual, Alleluya* (or *Tract*), *Gloria, Sanctus* and *Benedictus, Agnus Dei*—and all other invariable parts of the Mass, whether sung or spoken. A setting of the Mass would be a setting of the Movements from the *Ordinary*, usually sung by the people and/or choir.

* O.U.P. publish arrangements of hymns for brass band, recorders, voices with harmonicas and strings, etc.

The choir may enter in procession, in which case they would be vested, and would arrive in their places before the procession of ministers and servers. Except in Lent and Advent, the organist would normally play before (and during) the entry of the choir, as opportunity offers. If the choir is not robed, they may go to their places independently (i.e. without a procession). In many churches the choir sings from the gallery or organ-loft at the back of the church.

The organist would stop playing as soon as the ministers have arrived at the High Altar, and the celebrant is ready to intone the *Asperges me*.

Notes for any chant sung by one of the ministers are not the responsibility of the organist—unless so requested. Responses to prayers and versicles are not, as a rule, accompanied.

Cantors (sometimes two or four) will always start various sections of the *Proper*. A cantor is always a member of the choir—usually a tenor or baritone.

Accompaniment. Ordinarily any Gregorian chant (plainsong) may be accompanied, except in Lent or Advent. (At these times, accompaniment is only allowed for the practical necessity of supporting the chant—no accompaniment is allowed during the last three days of Holy Week.)

Preparation. In preparation for the Mass, the service opens on Sundays with the *Asperges me* (or in Paschal times (Easter) *Vidi Aquam*). This is started by the celebrant and continued by the choir and/or people. It is followed by three verses and responses (sung by the priest, answered by the people and/or choir), and a short prayer, after which the *introit* begins at once.

Introit (Variable)	(1) *Antiphon*—usually sets the mood of the day (dependent on the Feast). (2) *Psalm*—one or two verses (from which the *Antiphon* is sometimes, though not always, taken). (3) *Gloria*—(Glory be to the Father, etc.). (4) *Antiphon*—repeated. On occasions when the *Asperges me* is not sung, sometimes further verses of the Psalms are inserted in pairs, each pair being followed by the *Antiphon*. The *Gloria Patri* followed by the *Antiphon* (i.e. (3) and (4) above) is then delayed till

Kyrie (Invariable)	Although the form never varies, it may be sung: (1) *Alternately*, by people and choir. (2) Wholly by the people. (3) *Or* wholly by the choir. It may be accompanied or not, depending on the setting.

the last pair. These extra psalm-verses may be needed to give extra time for the entry procession of the ministers in a larger church.

Kyrie (Invariable) — Although the form never varies, it may be sung: (1) *Alternately*, by people and choir. (2) Wholly by the people. (3) *Or* wholly by the choir. It may be accompanied or not, depending on the setting.

Gloria (Invariable) (follows *Kyrie* immediately) — Organist would give the whole of the first phrase for the celebrant. The *Gloria* is rather long for the people to sing throughout, so it is usually divided between people and choir (phrase by phrase). Alternatively, it may be sung throughout by the choir. This could take as much as five or six minutes.

Collect(s) (Variable) (sung by celebrant) — Final amen(s) sung by people and/or choir. (Never more than two amens, though there can be three collects. The amens are for the first and last.) These are sung unaccompanied, and consist of two notes of equal value; the actual notes used depend on the Tone used for the prayer. (The setting used, and the number of prayers and amens will apply also to the *Prayer over the offerings* and the *Post-Communion Prayer*.)

Epistle (Variable) — Sung in Latin, or said in the Vernacular, by the celebrant, subdeacon, or reader.

Gradual *Alleluya* (or *Tract*) — Organist would give first few notes to introduce the first phrase for the cantors.

Sequence (Variable) (if prescribed) — This is always sung by the choir; the cantors singing the verse, and the choir concluding it. *Gradual*. Omitted from Low Sunday to Whit week inclusive, and replaced by an *Alleluya* (i.e. during Paschal times, there are two *Alleluyas*). *Alleluya*. This follows the *Gradual* (or in Paschal times, the first *Alleluya*). But in Lent it is replaced by the *Tract*).

To summarise:
Normally: Gradual, Alleluya.
Septuagesima–Holy Week: Gradual, Tract.
(inclusive)
Low Sunday–Whit Week: Alleluya, Alleluya.
(inclusive)
Sequence. There are five *Sequences*; these are only sung at the five prescribed times.

Gospel
(Variable)

Sung in Latin, or said in the Vernacular by the deacon (High Mass) or celebrant (*Missa Cantata*). This is followed by *Notices* and *Sermon.*

Nicene Creed
(Invariable)

Always sung every Sunday in the same way as the *Gloria.* Polyphonic settings are seldom performed.
The *Prayer of the Faithful* (Bidding Prayer) follows at once.

Offertory
(Variable)

As soon as the prayers are finished, the organist gives the introduction for the offertory, which consists of a few verses of sacred Scriptures. These are always sung by the choir.

Motet

This may follow if time allows. Occasionally a polyphonic setting of the *Offertory* may replace both Gregorian *Offertory* and *Motet.*

Prayer over offerings
(Variable)

This is sung by the celebrant after he has washed his fingers, returned to the centre of the Altar, invoked the Blessed Trinity, and turned towards the people and asked them to join with him in offering the Sacrifice. It concludes with amen sung by people and/or choir, and leads at once into:

Preface
(Variable according to season, not day by day)

The Preface. (1) *Versicles* and *Responses*, sung by the celebrant, answered by the people and/or choir. (2) *Main Text* is then continued by the celebrant. At the end of the Preface, celebrant and choir pursue their separate ways, simultaneously.

184

| And *Canon* with *Sanctus-Benedictus* (Invariable) | *Canon* (spoken by celebrant) The *Canon* is a series of prayers, spoken silently by the celebrant. | *Sanctus and Benedictus* (sung by choir) (*a*) *Gregorian Setting.* While the celebrant says the *Canon*, the *Sanctus* and *Benedictus* are sung without separation by people and/or choir. (*b*) *Alternatively*, if a polyphonic setting is used, *Sanctus* only is sung, by the choir. |
| | The central climax is the: | This ends at the: |

| *Consecration* (Central point of the Mass) | | |
| | After which the *Canon* continues. | If (*b*) above, *Benedictus* follows here, sung by the choir. If (*a*) above, all remain silent. |

Pater Noster (Invariable)

The *Pater Noster* section of the Mass includes four parts:
(1) The celebrant concludes aloud (to the set chant) the final prayer of the *Canon* (which began after the *Preface*, above) to which the people and/or choir respond with a sung amen.
(2) The celebrant sings the introduction to the *Pater Noster* (*Preceptis . . . dicere*) and for the prayer itself is joined by the people and/or choir.
(3) After the *Pater Noster* (no amen) the celebrant sings another prayer; the people and/or choir answer amen.
(4) The celebrant then sings the versicle "*Pax Domini sit semper vobiscum*"; the people and/or choir respond "*Et cum spirito Tuo*".

Agnus Dei (Invariable)	This is followed immediately by: Sung by the people and/or choir.
Communion (Variable)	Soon after the *Agnus Dei*, the choir and people receive Holy Communion. Various chants may be sung during this time by the people and/or choir (e.g. a hymn, a setting of a psalm—e.g. Gélineau—or an anthem or motet), but the Communion antiphon for the day must be sung before the celebrant is ready to sing the Post-Communion Prayer. A good moment to sing the antiphon is as soon as the people's Communion has begun: at latest it may be begun immediately after the distribution of Holy Communion has finished. The antiphon may also be used between verses of psalms sung at this point to a plainsong setting. In this event, the psalms must be sung in the mode of the antiphon.
Postcommunion (Variable)	After the celebrant has purified the chalice and veiled it, he kisses the Altar, turns to the people and sings *"Dominus vobiscum"*, to which the people and/or choir respond *"Et cum spiritu tuo"*. The celebrant then sings the Postcommunion Prayers, at the end of which the people and/or choir respond "Amen". The celebrant sings *"Dominus vobiscum"*: the people and/or choir respond *"Et cum spiritu tuo"*. The deacon (High Mass) or celebrant (Low Mass) sings *"Ite Missa Est"* to one of the set chants, by previous arrangement with the organist or choirmaster. (There are many of these chants to choose from.) The people and/or choir respond *"Deo Gratias"*. This is followed immediately by the blessing, given by the celebrant (spoken).

This line signifies the end of the Mass. The *Prayer for the Sovereign* follows at once; this consists of a versicle sung by the celebrant

> *"Domine, salvam fac*
> *Reginam nostram, N . . ."*
> *Regem nostrum, N . . ."*

to which the people and/or choir respond: "*Et exaudi nos in die que invocaverimus te.*" In some places this may all take the form of a short motet. In either form it is followed by the prayer "*Quaesumas' omnipotens Deus*", at the conclusion of which the people and/or choir respond "Amen". This concludes the service, and the *Recessional*, whether sung or played, may be begun.

(The approximate length of the service will normally be an hour to an hour-and-a-quarter.)

ABBREVIATIONS AND EXPLANATION OF TERMS

℣ $= \begin{cases} \text{Versicle} \\ \text{Verse} \end{cases}$ sung by individuals — e.g. celebrant or cantors.

R℣   = Response sung by the people and/or choir.

*   = Cantor stops and choir resumes (in all but psalmody).

*ij   = is found in *Alleluyas*, and denotes: cantors sing from beginning to star as usual; choir then repeats cantor's phrase and carries on to the end of the word. (The notes after the asterisk are always sung on the final syllable of *Alleluya*.)

iij   = sing three times (only applies to plainsong *Kyries*, i.e. *Ninefold Kyrie*).

Tone = Tune (at its simplest). When applied to psalms, tones are grouped (with one or two exceptions) under each of the eight modes: they vary in their ending.

Mode = The mode of a piece. This is always indicated by a number at the beginning (e.g. Intr. 4 = introit, fourth mode). There were originally four modes ending on r.m.f.s. These became eight: 1, 3, 5, 7 being high settings; 2, 4, 6, 8 being low settings — otherwise the two sets corresponded to each other. (Chapter Two contains more information on the modes.)

THE FREE CHURCH (NONCOMFORMIST) TRADITION

Since many of the Free Churches are more or less non-liturgical in their mode of worship, their orders of service are, not surprisingly, more flexible than those of the Church of England.

Bearing in mind that there are many local variations, it may nevertheless be interesting to compare the order of Morning Service in a single church (chosen at random) in each of four different denominations.

Baptist	Congregational	Methodist	Presbyterian
Scripture sentences	Introit	Introit	Call to Worship
Short prayer and The Lord's Prayer (spoken)	Silent adoration	Scripture Sentences Hymn	Hymn
Hymn	Invocation	Invocation and Confession	Prayers of Confession, Petition, and The Lord's Prayer
Reading	General thanksgiving	The Lord's Prayer (spoken or sung)	Lesson (Old Testament)
Children's Address	Hymn	Chant or hymn	Metrical Psalm
	Lesson (Old Testament)		
Children's hymn	Children's hymn	Lesson (Old Testament)	Lesson (New Testament)
Offering	Lesson (New Testament)	Children's Address	Hymn
Hymn	Anthem	Children's hymn	Prayers of Intercession
Prayer	Silent Fellowship (prayers) The Lord's Prayer (spoken)	Lesson (New Testament)	Hymn
Sermon	Sermon	Prayers	Sermon
Hymn	Offertory	Anthem	Offering and Dedication
Benediction	Prayer of Dedication	Offertory	Hymn
	Hymn	Hymn	Benediction (and sung amen)
	Benediction (and sung amen)	Sermon	
		Hymn Benediction	

Evening services are on similar lines, the hymn for children being of course replaced by one for adults. In Free Churches, the sacrament of Holy Communion is usually observed less frequently than in the Church of England (e.g. once a month in the Presbyterian Church, and twice a month in the Baptist Church may perhaps be said to be normal).

The Communion Service, whether combined with (e.g. Presbyterian), or following (e.g. Baptist) the normal Morning or Evening Service, has usually little special music, apart from Communion hymns.

The British Province of the Moravian Church, a province of the oldest Free Church in Northern Europe, has one liturgical service each Sunday (usually the Morning Service), which is chosen from orders (one to six) from the Moravian Liturgy.

THE SALVATION ARMY

Sunday worship, traditionally, takes three forms which, to some extent, reflect the Methodist background of the founder, William Booth. From the earliest days music, singing and brass bands have been a vital part of the Army. Salvationists have written, composed and arranged most of the Army's music. The brass bands have always consisted solely of Army members who pay for their own uniforms, receive no fee for their services, and agree strictly to observe the rules and regulations authorised by the General. There are also Songster Brigades of male and female adult singers, bands and "singing companies" for young people and, occasionally, string, concertina and timbrel bands.

The Sunday morning "Holiness" meeting (for spiritual development, teaching, etc.) opens with a "song" (hymn) of the adoration type; this is the only song accompanied by the band, which is not permitted to play thereafter. Prayer follows, with perhaps a sung chorus of a reflective or devotional character; then a second song—perhaps by the singing company of young people—which is accompanied by a piano, harmonium or electric organ. After a Bible Reading and "Witness", the Songster Brigade may sing an anthem or gospel song. The offering is followed by an address, and the meeting closes with a final song, often of an introspective or challenging nature.

The Sunday afternoon service takes several forms, the basis being "Praise". The band may render an item or two of a festive nature, and the Songster Brigade an anthem or bright song, and perhaps also a quieter song or hymn tune arrangement, usually with piano or organ accompaniment. There may be talks from visitors or missionaries, and a short Bible talk. The whole service is a mixture of witness, congregational singing, solos, band items, and so on. This stems from the early Christian mission days of witness or "testimony" meetings, in which the members of the congregation have the opportunity to express, individually, some incident or experiences relating to their spiritual life; this is similar to the "sharing" in Moral Rearmament.

The Sunday evening "Salvation" meeting is designed to have an outward thrust. The pattern is similar to that of the morning meeting, except that the band takes part as a solo unit. There may be a rhythm group song, but this is rare; rhythm groups, such as the "Joy Strings", more often play in coffee bars, youth clubs, etc. The nature of the music is usually addressed to the unconverted, but "experience" songs are also included. The songs are chosen to fit the theme of the meeting or the address. Following the Salvation meeting there is a short prayer meeting at which songs or choruses with a definite challenge are used, together with prayer and exhortation. Sometimes the day is rounded off with a "Wind-up" meeting, which is a kind of "rejoicing" service ("winding-up" the day), where the musical sections participate and testimonies are offered; but this meeting is dying out in many places.

BIBLIOGRAPHY

(A selection of books on various aspects of Church music)

GENERAL

Cleall, Charles, *Music and Holiness* (Epworth Press)

Davidson, A. Y., *Church Music—Illusion or Reality* (Harvard–O.U.P.)

Davies, Walford, & Grace, Harvey, *Music and Worship* (Eyre & Spottiswoode)

Dearmer, Percy, *The Parson's Handbook*, 13th edition (1965) revised by the Revd. Cyril E. Pocknee (O.U.P.)

Douglas, Winifred, *Church Music in History and Practice* (Faber & Faber)

Fellowes, E. H., *English Cathedral Music* (Methuen)

Nicholson, Sydney, *Quires and Places Where They Sing* (S.P.C.K.)

Phillips, C. Henry, *The Singing Church* (Faber & Faber)

Routley, Erik, *Church Music and Theology* (Waltham Forest Books)

Routley, Erik, *Twentieth Century Church Music* (Herbert Jenkins)

Spence, Horace, *Praises with Understanding* (R.S.C.M.)

(A handbook for ordinands and the clergy, which is also of interest to the Church musician.)

CHOIR TRAINING, ETC.

Bostock, Donald, *Choirmastery* (Epworth Press)

Coleman, Henry, *The Church Choir-Trainer* (O.U.P.)

Long, Kenneth R., *Church Choir Management* (Faith Press)

Mellalieu, W. N., *The Boy's Changing Voice* (O.U.P.)

Moody, C. H., *The Choirboy in the Making* (O.U.P.)

Morgan, S. M., *Choirs in Little Churches* (Faith Press)

Sims, M. A., *Sight-Reading for Choirboys* (Nov., Music Primer No. 118)

Vale, S. M., *The Training of Boys' Voices* (Faith Press)

Wright, Edred, *Basic Choir Training* (R.S.C.M.)

Alcock, Walter G., *The Organ* (Nov., Music Primer No. 88)

Buck, Percy C., *The First Year at the Organ* (S. & B.)

Coleman, Henry, *The Amateur Organist* (O.U.P.)

Conway, M. P., *Playing a Church Organ* (Canterbury Press)

Conway, M. P., *Church Organ Accompaniment* (Canterbury Press)

Hinrichsen, Max (editor), *Organ and Choral Aspects and Prospects* (Hinrichsen Edition)

Lang, C. S., *Exercises for Organists* (Nov., Music Primers Nos. 128 & 129)
   (Sight Reading, Transposition, etc. Book 1 for A.R.C.O.; Book 2 for F.R.C.O.)

Phillips, C. Henry, *Modern Organ Pedalling* (O.U.P.)

Routley, Erik, *The Organist's Guide to Congregational Praise* (Independent Press)

Sumner, W. L., *The Organ* (Macdonald)

Thiman, Eric, *The Beginning Organist* (Ascherberg)

Thiman, Eric, *Improvisation on Hymn Tunes* (Nov., Music Primer No. 135)

Tobin, J. R., *Figured-Bass Playing* (Nov., Music Primer No. 79)

Watson, J. T., *How to Play a Hymn Tune* (Epworth Press)

Various authors, *The Organist and the Congregation* (Independent Press)
   (Lectures and a Sermon delivered at the first Conference of Congregational Organists, in 1951.)

Novello publish several books (by C. S. Lang) of Paperwork Tests, Score-reading Exercises, etc., of A.R.C.O. and F.R.C.O. standard.

PLAINSONG

Apel, Willi, *Gregorian Chant* (Burnes & Oates)

Arnold, J. H., *The Approach to Plainsong Through the Office Hymn* (O.U.P.)

Arnold, J. H., *Plainsong Accompaniment* (Waltham Forest Books)

Briggs, H. B., & Frere, W. H., revised and enlarged by J. H. Arnold, *A Manual of Plainsong* (Nov.)
   (A most useful book containing the whole Psalter, all the Canticles, the Litany, Merbecke's Communion, all pointed and set to plainsong, for use with the Book of Common Prayer.)

Burgess, Francis, *The Teaching and Accompaniment of Plainsong* (Nov.)

Murray, Gregory, *Gregorian Chant* (Cary)

Snelders, Philip, *A Beginner's Plainsong* (Fowler Wright Books)

Vale, Walter S., *Plainsong* (Faith Press)

ROMAN CATHOLIC CHURCH MUSIC

Buckley, Kevin, *A Handbook for Catholic Choirmasters and Organists* (Cary)

Edeson, Donald J. S., *The Training of Catholic Choirs* (Cary)

Gélineau, Joseph, trans. Clifford Howells, *Voices and Instruments in Christian Worship* (Burns & Oates)

Robertson, Alec, *Music of the Catholic Church* (Burns & Oates)

PSALMS

Lamb, J. A., *The Psalms in Christian Worship* (Faith Press)

Lloyd, Philip, *Reading on the Psalms* (Mowbray)

Phillips, C. S., *A Little Companion to the Psalter* (S.P.C.K.)

CAROLS

Nettel, Reginald, *Christmas and its Carols* (Faith Press)

Routley, Erik, *The English Carol* (Herbert Jenkins)

APPENDIX TWO

100 STIRRING TUNES

No two musicians would produce an exactly similar list. This is offered in the hope that it may form a basis, which the reader can add to, or subtract from, until he has a working selection agreeable to his own taste. He might even be encouraged to prepare a completely different list of his own. These tunes may be useful for giving a service or occasion a good start or finish. They are only a selection. There is, in fact, a lack of four-line tunes—tunes such as *Carlisle, Gerontious, Old Hundredth, Richmond, St. Denio, Truro, Winchester New & Old*, produce a confident roar from the congregation; but in the present writers' opinion they are not as stirring as some of the broader tunes listed in the table.

100 STIRRING TUNES

(When a number is in brackets, the words are fitted to another tune, or the tune has different words.)

First Line	Tune	A. & M. Rev.	S. of P.	E.H.	M.H.
Alleluya, alleluya	Lux Eoi	137	(150)	(127)	(706)
Alleluya, sing to Jesus	Hyfrydol	399	260	301	(380)
All glory, laud and honour	St. Theodulph	98	135	622	84
All hail the power of	Miles Lane	217	440	364	91
All the toil and sorrow done	Llanfair	(147)	149	(143)	(205)
All things bright and beautiful	Royal Oak	442	444	587	851
And did those feet	Jerusalem	578	446	—	(v.1)
Angels from the realms	Iris	(594)	71	—	119
Angel voices ever singing	Angel voices	246	—	—	668
A safe stronghold	Ein' Feste Burg	183	436	362	494
Be still my soul	Finlandia	(Ch. Hymnary 556)			
Christian dost thou see them	St. Andrew of Crete	91	(466)	(72)	—

194

First Line	Tune	A. & M. Rev.	S. of P.	E.H.	M.H.
Christ is the world's true light	Rinkart	—	60	—	—
Christ the Lord is risen again	Orientis Partibus	(524)	153	129	(207) (87)
Come ye faithful	Neander	222	477	380	(53)
Come ye thankful people	St. George (Elvey)	482	9	289	962
Crown him with many crowns	Diademata	224	(480)	(381)	271
Dear Lord and Father	Repton	184	481	383	(669)
Far round the world	Woodlands	—	299	—	(798)
Fight the good fight	Duke Street	304	491	(389)	(784)
For all the Saints	Sine Nomine	—	202	641	832
For ever with the Lord	Nearer Home	346	(195)	App. 51	658
Glorious things of thee	Austria	257	500	393	(706)
God is love	Theodoric	—	502	—	—
God is working his purpose out	Benson	271	(300)	App. 63	(812)
God rest you, merry	God rest you	(Meth. School H.B. 525)			
Good Christian men	Gelobt sei Gott (Vulpius)	603	154	—	(143)
Guide me, O thou great	Cwm Rhondda	296	(508)	(397)	615
Hail, the day that sees	Chislehurst	610	(172)	(143)	(221)
	Llanfair	147	(172)	143	(221)
	Ascension	147	(172)	(143)	221
Hail to the Lord's anointed	Crüger (Herrnhut)	219	87	45	245
Hark the Herald	Mendelssohn (Bethlehem)	60	74	24	117
He who would valiant be	Monks Gate	—	515	402	620
Hills of the North	Little Cornard	269	64	—	815
Holy, holy, holy	Nicaea	160	187	162	36
How brightly beams	Morgenstern	—	90	—	—
How great the harvest	Vruechten	—	169	—	—
I bind unto myself	St. Patrick	162	528	212	392
I hear Thy welcome voice	Welcome Voice (Ch. Hymnary 689)	—	—	573	351
In the name of Jesus	Cuddesdon	(Ch. Hymnary 178)			
I think when I read	Endearment (Meth. Sch. H.B. 143)	—	—	(595)	(865)
I vow to thee, my country	Thaxted	579	319	—	900

First Line	Tune	A. & M. Rev.	S. of P.	E.H.	M.H.
Jerusalem on High	Christchurch	280	197	411	(653)
Jerusalem the golden	Ewing	278	198	412	(652)
Jesu, Lover of my soul	Aberystwyth	(86)	542	414	(110)
Jesus Christ is risen	Easter Hymn	134	145	133	(204)
Jesus lives!	St. Albinus	140	155	134	216
King of Glory	Gwalchmai	367	553	424	23
Let all the world	⌠Universal Praise	(375)	(556)	427	(5)
	⌡Luckington	375	(556)	(427)	5
Let us rejoice	Easter Song	(172)	157	(519)	(4)
Let us with a gladsome	Monkland	377	12	532	(19)
Lift high the cross	Crucifer	633	—	—	—
Lift up your voice	Ladywell	297	—	—	—
Light's abode	Regent Square	279	(199)	431	(12)
Lo he comes with clouds	Helmsley	51	65	7	264
Lord of our life	Iste Confessor (Rouen)	253	349	435	(729)
Lo when the day	Hermann	(609)	159	—	(222)
Mine eyes have seen	⌠Battle Hymn	—	(578)	—	260
	⌡Battle Song	—	578	—	(260)
Now thank we all	Nun Danket	379	350	533	10
O come all ye faithful	Adeste Fideles	59	78	614	118
O come, O come, Immanuel	Veni Immanuel	49	66	8	257
O God of earth	Kings Lynn	—	308	562	—
O happy band of pilgrims	Kocher (Knecht)	289	(599)	452	618
O Jesus I have promised	Thornbury	(256)	255	(577)	(526)
O Love of God	O amor quam exstaticus	—	607	(214)	(52)
Once to every man	Ebenezer	—	309	(563)	(898)
Onward! Christian Soldiers	St. Gertrude	629	(397)	643	822
O praise ye the Lord	Laudate Dominum	376	351	—	(426)
O son of man	Londonderry	—	611	—	(241)
O worship the King	Hanover	167	618	466	8
O worship the Lord	Was lebet	77	(93)	42	(9)
Praise, my soul	Praise, my soul	365	623	470	12
Praise to the Lord	Lobe den Herren	382	626	536	64
Rejoice, the Lord is King	Gopsal	216	632	476	247
Shepherds in the fields	Shepherds in the Fields	594	71	—	(119)
Sing Alleluya	St. Sebastian (Martins)	283	247	—	(671)
Sing all good people	Ellacombe	132	193	(137)	(208)
Soldiers of Christ	St. Ethelwald	303	641	479	(484)

First Line	Tune	A. & M. Rev.	S. of P.	E.H.	M.H.
Stand up, stand up!	Morning Light	307	646	581	821
Ten thousand times	Alford	284	—	(486)	828
The Church's one foundation	Aurelia	255	249	489	701
The first Nowell	First Nowell	—	384	—	131
The God of Abraham praise	Leoni	631	398	646	21
The holy Son of God	Von Himmel Hoch	—	80	(17)	(42)
The Lord of Heaven confess	Croft's 136th	(248)	657	(565)	(26)
The Lord will come	Psalm 107	(Ch. Hymnary 151)			
The strife is o'er	Victory	135	147	625	215
Thine be the Glory	Maccabaeus	—	—	—	213
Thou didst leave	Margaret	363	—	585	150
Thou whose almighty	Moscow	266	303	553	(803)
Through the night	Marching	(182)	678	503 App.	616
To Thee, O Lord	Golden Sheaves	484	(13)	17	964
To Thee our God	Croft's 148th Croft's 136th	606	(657)	565	(886)
Trumpet of God	Rangoon	270	—	—	—
Wake, O wake	Sleepers Wake	(55)	687	12	255
Welcome Day of the Lord	Salve Festa Dies	—	390	(624)	—
We plough the fields	Wir pflügen	483	14	293	963
When morning gilds the skies	Laudes Domini	223	—	—	113
Who are these like stars	All Saints	570	210	204	(100)
Ye holy angels bright	Darwalls 148th	371	701	517	(26)
Ye sons and daughters	O filii et filiae	130	143	626	—

A few of the above tunes have alternative names in the different hymn books.

Crofts 136th = Crofts 148th
Crüger = Herrnhut
Easter Hymn = Easter Morn
Easter Song = Easter Alleluya = Lasst uns Erfreuen = St. Francis
Ein' Feste Burg = A Stronghold Sure
Gelobt sei Gott = Vulpius
Hermann = Erschienen ist
Iris = Shepherds in the Fields
Jerusalem (E.H.) is different from Parry's tune

Kocher = Knecht
Lobe den Herren = Praxis pietatis = Hast du denn, Jesu
Mendelssohn = Berlin = Bethlehem
Montgomery (E.H.) = Nearer Home
(There is another *Montgomery* tune which is quite different)
Neander = Unser Herrscher
O Seigneur = Psalm 3
Sleepers Wake = Wachet Auf
St. Sebastian = Martins
Welcome Voice = Calvary (M.H.)

INDEX